Stand Out 3

Standards-Based English

Second Edition

Staci Johnson

Rob Jenkins

HEINLE
CENGAGE Learning

Australia • Brazil • Japan • Korea • Mexico • Singapore • Spain • United Kingdom • United States

**Stand Out 3: Standards-Based English,
Second Edition**
Staci Johnson and Rob Jenkins

Editorial Director: Joe Dougherty

Publisher, ESL and Dictionaries: Sherrise Roehr

Acquisitions Editor: Tom Jefferies

VP, Director of Content Development: Anita
Raducanu

Developmental Editor: John Hicks

Associate Media Development Editor: Jonelle
Lonergan

Director of Product Marketing: Amy T. Mabley

Executive Marketing Manager, U.S.: Jim
McDonough

Senior Field Marketing Manager: Donna Lee
Kennedy

Product Marketing Manager: Katie Kelley

Content Project Manager: Dawn Marie Elwell

Senior Print Buyer: Mary Beth Hennebury

Developmental Editor: Kasia McNabb

Project Manager: Tunde Dewey

Composition: Pre-Press PMG

Cover and Interior Design: Studio Montage

Cover Art: ©Lisa Henderling/Getty Images

Photo Researcher: Erika Hokanson

Illustrators: James Edwards; S.I. International

Credits appear on page 176, which constitutes a
continuation of the copyright page.

For product information and technology assistance, contact us at
Cengage Learning Customer & Sales Support, 1-800-354-9706

For permission to use material from this text or product,
submit all requests online at **www.cengage.com/permissions**
Further permissions questions can be emailed to
permissionrequest@cengage.com

Library of Congress Control Number: 2007905341

Student Edition

ISBN-13: 978-1-4240-0260-3

ISBN-10: 1-4240-0260-5

Heinle
20 Channel Center Street
Boston, MA 02210
USA

Cengage Learning is a leading provider of customized learning solutions with
office locations around the globe, including Singapore, the United Kingdom,
Australia, Mexico, Brazil, and Japan. Locate your local office at:
international.cengage.com/region

Cengage Learning products are represented in Canada by Nelson Education, Ltd.

Visit Heinle online at **elt.heinle.com**

Visit our corporate website at **cengage.com**

Printed in the United States of America
5 6 7 12

Elizabeth Aderman
New York City Board of Education, New York, NY

Sharon Baker
Roseville Adult School, Roseville, CA

Lillian Barredo
Stockton School for Adults, Stockton, CA

Linda Boice
Elk Grove Adult Education, Elk Grove, CA

Chan Bostwick
Los Angeles Unified School District, Los Angeles, CA

Debra Brooks
Manhattan BEGIN Program, New York, NY

Anne Byrnes
North Hollywood-Polytechnic Community Adult School, Sun Valley, CA

Rose Cantu
John Jay High School, San Antonio, TX

Toni Chapralis
Fremont School for Adults, Sacramento, CA

Melanie Chitwood
Miami-Dade College, Miami, FL

Geri Creamer
Stockton School for Adults, Stockton, CA

Stephanie Daubar
Harry W. Brewster Technical Center, Tampa, FL

Irene Dennis
San Antonio College, San Antonio, TX

Eileen Duffell
P.S. 64, New York, NY

Nancy Dunlap
Northside Independent School District, San Antonio, TX

Gloria Eriksson
Grant Skills Center, Sacramento, CA

Marti Estrin
Santa Rosa Junior College, Santa Rosa, CA

Lawrence Fish
Shorefront YM-YWHA English Language Program, Brooklyn, NY

Victoria Florit
Miami-Dade College, Miami, FL

Rhoda Gilbert
New York City Board of Education, New York, NY

Kathleen Jimenez
Miami-Dade College, Miami, FL

Nancy Jordan
John Jay High School Adult Education, San Antonio, TX

Renee Klosz
Lindsey Hopkins Technical Education Center, Miami, FL

David Lauter
Stockton School for Adults, Stockton, CA

Patricia Long
Old Marshall Adult Education Center, Sacramento, CA

Daniel Loos
Seattle Community College, Seattle, WA

Maria Miranda
Lindsey Hopkins Technical Education Center, Miami, FL

Karen Moore
Stockton School for Adults, Stockton, CA

George Myskiw
Malcolm X College, Chicago, IL

Heidi Perez
Lawrence Public Schools Adult Learning Center, Lawrence, MA

Marta Pitt
Lindsey Hopkins Technical Education Center, Miami, FL

Sylvia Rambach
Stockton School for Adults, Stockton, CA

Eric Rosenbaum
BEGIN Managed Programs, New York, NY

Laura Rowley
Old Marshall Adult Education Center, Sacramento, CA

Stephanie Schmitter
Mercer County Community College, Trenton, NJ

Amy Schneider
Pacoima Skills Center, Pacoima, CA

Sr. M. B. Theresa Spittle
Stockton School for Adults, Stockton, CA

Andre Sutton
Belmont Adult School, Los Angeles, CA

Jennifer Swoyer
Northside Independent School District, San Antonio, TX

Claire Valier
Palm Beach County School District, West Palm Beach, FL

Staci Johnson

Rob Jenkins

Ever since I can remember, I've been fascinated with other cultures and languages. I love to travel and every place I go, the first thing I want to do is meet the people, learn their language, and understand their culture. Becoming an ESL teacher was a perfect way to turn what I love to do into my profession. There's nothing more incredible than the exchange of teaching and learning from one another that goes on in an ESL classroom. And there's nothing more rewarding than helping a student succeed.

I love teaching. I love to see the expressions on my students' faces when the light goes on and their eyes show such sincere joy of learning. I knew the first time I stepped into an ESL classroom that this was where I needed to be and I have never questioned that resolution. I have worked in business, sales, and publishing, and I've found challenge in all, but nothing can compare to the satisfaction of reaching people in such a personal way.

We are so happy that instructors and agencies have embraced the lesson planning and project-based activities that we introduced in the first edition and are so enthusiastically teaching with **Stand Out**. It is fantastic that so many of our colleagues are as excited to be in this profession as we are. After writing over 500 lesson plans and implementing them in our own classrooms and after personal discussions with thousands of instructors all over the United States and in different parts of the world, we have found ourselves in a position to improve upon our successful model. One of the most notable things in the new edition is that we have continued to stress integrating skills in each lesson and have made this integration more apparent and obvious. To accomplish any life skill, students need to incorporate a combination of reading, writing, listening, speaking, grammar, pronunciation, and academic skills while developing vocabulary and these skills should be taught together in a lesson! We have accomplished this by extending the presentation of lessons in the book, so each lesson is more fully developed. You will also notice an extended list of ancillaries and a tighter correlation of these ancillaries to each book. The ancillaries allow you to extend practice on particular skill areas beyond the lesson in the text. We are so excited about this curriculum and know that as you implement it, you and your students will *stand out*.

Our goal is to give students
challenging opportunities
to be successful in their
language-learning experience
so they develop confidence
and become independent,
lifelong learners.

Staci Johnson
Rob Jenkins

ABOUT THE SERIES

The **Stand Out** series is designed to facilitate *active* learning while challenging students to build a nurturing and effective learning community.

The student books are divided into eight distinct units, mirroring competency areas most useful to newcomers. These areas are outlined in CASAS assessment programs and different state model standards for adults. Each unit in *Stand Out 3* is then divided into five lessons, a review, and a team project. Lessons are driven by performance objectives and are filled with challenging activities that progress from teacher-presented to student-centered tasks.

SUPPLEMENTAL MATERIALS

- The *Stand Out 3 Lesson Planner* is in full color with 60 complete lesson plans, taking the instructor through each stage of a lesson from warm-up and review through application.

- The *Stand Out 3 Activity Bank CD-ROM* has an abundance of customizable worksheets. Print or download and modify what you need for your particular class.

- The *Stand Out 3 Grammar Challenge* is a workbook that gives additional grammar explanation and practice in context.

- The *Reading and Writing Challenge* workbooks are designed to capture the principle ideas in the student book, and allow students to improve their vocabulary, academic, reading, and writing skills.

- The *Stand Out 3 Assessment CD-ROM with ExamView®* allows you to customize pre- and post-tests for each unit as well as a pre- and post-test for the book.

- Listening scripts are found in the back of the student book and in the Lesson Planner. CDs are available with focused listening activities described in the Lesson Planner.

STAND OUT 3 LESSON PLANNER

The *Stand Out 3 Lesson Planner* is a new and innovative approach. As many seasoned teachers know, good lesson planning can make a substantial difference in the classroom. Students continue coming to class, understanding, applying, and remembering more of what they learn. They are more confident in their learning when good lesson planning techniques are incorporated.

We have developed lesson plans that are designed to be used each day and to reduce preparation time. The planner includes:

- Standard lesson progression (Warm-up and Review, Introduction, Presentation, Practice, Evaluation, and Application)

- A creative and complete way to approach varied class lengths so that each lesson will work within a class period.
- 180 hours of classroom activities
- Time suggestions for each activity
- Pedagogical comments
- Space for teacher notes and future planning
- Identification of LCP standards in addition to SCANS and CASAS standards

USER QUESTIONS ABOUT *STAND OUT*

- **What are SCANS and how do they integrate into the book?**
  SCANS is the Secretary's Commission on Achieving Necessary Skills. SCANS was developed to encourage students to prepare for the workplace. The standards developed through SCANS have been incorporated throughout the **Stand Out** student books and components.

  Stand Out addresses SCANS a little differently than do other books. SCANS standards elicit effective teaching strategies by incorporating essential skills such as critical thinking and group work. We have incorporated SCANS standards in every lesson, not isolating these standards in the work unit. All new texts have followed our lead.

- **What about CASAS?** The federal government has mandated that states show student outcomes as a prerequisite to receiving funding. Some states have incorporated the **C**omprehensive **A**dult **S**tudent **A**ssessment **S**ystem (CASAS) testing to standardize agency reporting. Unfortunately, many of our students are unfamiliar with standardized testing and therefore struggle with it. Adult schools need to develop lesson plans to address specific concerns. **Stand Out** was developed with careful attention to CASAS skill areas in most lessons and performance objectives.

- **Are the tasks too challenging for my students?**
  Students learn by doing and learn more when challenged. **Stand Out** provides tasks that encourage critical thinking in a variety of ways. The tasks in each lesson move from teacher-directed to student-centered so the learner clearly understands what's expected and is willing to "take a risk." The lessons are expected to be challenging. In this way, students learn that when they work together as a learning community, anything becomes possible. The satisfaction of accomplishing something both as an individual and as a member of a team results in greater confidence and effective learning.

- **Do I need to understand lesson planning to teach from the student book?** If you don't understand lesson planning when you start, you will when you finish! Teaching from **Stand Out** is like a course on lesson planning, especially if you use the Lesson Planner on a daily basis.

  Stand Out does *stand out* because, when we developed this series, we first established performance objectives for each lesson. Then we designed lesson plans, followed by student book pages. The introduction to each lesson varies because different objectives demand different approaches. **Stand Out's** variety of tasks makes learning more interesting for the student.

- **What are team projects?** The final lesson of each unit is a **team project**. This is often a team simulation that incorporates the objectives of the unit and provides an additional opportunity for students to actively apply what they have learned. The project allows students to produce something that represents their progress in learning. These end-of-unit projects were created with a variety of learning styles and individual skills in mind. The team projects can be skipped or simplified, but we encourage instructors to implement them, enriching the overall student experience.

- **What do you mean by a customizable Activity Bank?** Every class, student, teacher, and approach is different. Since no one textbook can meet all these differences, the *Stand Out Activity Bank CD-ROM* allows you to customize **Stand Out** for your class. You can copy different activities and worksheets from the CD-ROM to your hard drive and then:

  - change items in supplemental vocabulary, grammar, and life skill activities;

  - personalize activities with student names and popular locations in your area;

  - extend every lesson with additional practice where you feel it is most needed.

  The Activity Bank also includes the following resources:

  - Multilevel worksheets – worksheets based on the standard worksheets described above, but at one level higher and one level lower.

  - Graphic organizer templates – templates that can be used to facilitate learning. They include graphs, charts, VENN diagrams, and so on.

  - Computer worksheets – worksheets designed to supplement each unit and progress from simple

  to complex operations in word processing; and spreadsheets for labs and computer enhanced classrooms.

  - Internet Worksheets – worksheets designed to supplement each unit and provide application opportunities beyond the lessons in the book.

- **Is *Stand Out* grammar-based or competency-based?** **Stand Out** is a competency-based series; however, students are exposed to basic grammar structures. We believe that grammar instruction in context is extremely important. Grammar is a necessary component for achieving most competencies; therefore it is integrated into most lessons. Students are first provided with context that incorporates the grammar, followed by an explanation and practice. At this level, we expect students to learn basic structures, but we do not expect them to acquire them. It has been our experience that students are exposed several times within their learning experience to language structures before they actually acquire them. For teachers who want to enhance grammar instruction, the *Activity Bank CD-ROM* and/or the *Grammar Challenge* workbooks provide ample opportunities.

  The six competencies that drive **Stand Out** are basic communication, consumer economics, community resources, health, occupational knowledge, and lifelong learning (government and law replace lifelong learning in Books 3 and 4).

- **Are there enough activities so I don't have to supplement?** **Stand Out** stands alone in providing 180 hours of instruction and activities, even without the additional suggestions in the Lesson Planner. The Lesson Planner also shows you how to streamline lessons to provide 90 hours of classwork and still have thorough lessons if you meet less often. When supplementing with the *Stand Out Activity Bank CD-ROM*, the *Assessment CD-ROM with ExamView®* and the *Stand Out Grammar Challenge* workbook, you gain unlimited opportunities to extend class hours and provide activities related directly to each lesson objective. Calculate how many hours your class meets in a semester and look to **Stand Out** to address the full class experience.

  Stand Out is a comprehensive approach to adult language learning, meeting needs of students and instructors completely and effectively.

CONTENTS

● Grammar points that are explicitly taught   ◊ Grammar points that are presented in context   △ Grammar points that are being recycled

	Numeracy/ Academic Skills	EFF	SCANS	CASAS
Pre-Unit	• Writing a paragraph • Comparing and contrasting • Setting goals	• Taking responsibility for learning • Reflecting and evaluating • Planning • Conveying ideas in writing	Many SCAN and EFF skills are incorporated in this unit with an emphasis on: • Understanding systems • Decision making	**1:** 0.1.2; 0.1.4; 0.2.1; 0.2.2 **2:** 0.2.1; 7.2.6 **3:** 0.1.2, 0.1.6, 0.2.1, 7.1.1
Unit 1	• Pronunciation • Reading a chart • Active reading • Focused listening • Writing a paragraph • Active reading • Making inferences • Using an outline • Using a pie graph • Reviewing	Most EFF skills are incorporated into this unit with an emphasis on: • Taking responsibility for learning • Using information and communication technology • Conveying ideas in writing • Solving problems and making decisions • Planning (Technology is optional.)	Many SCAN and EFF skills are incorporated in this unit with an emphasis on: • Allocating time • Understanding systems • Applying technology to task • Responsibility • Self management • Writing • Decision making	**1:** 0.1.2, 0.2.4 **2:** 7.1.1, 7.1.2, 7.1.3, 7.2.5, 7.2.6 **3:** 7.1.1, 7.1.2, 7.1.3, 7.2.5, 7.2.6 **4:** 0.1.5, 7.4.1, 7.4.3, 7.4.5 **5:** 7.4.2 **R:** 7.2.1 **TP:** 4.8.1., 4.8.5., 4.8.6.
Unit 2	• Pronunciation: Focus • Test taking skills • Comparing and contrasting • Sequence writing • Reviewing	Most EFF skills are incorporated into this unit with an emphasis on: • Reflecting and evaluating • Learning through research • Cooperating with others • Solving problems and making decisions. (Technology is optional.)	Many SCAN skills are incorporated in this unit with an emphasis on: • Responsibility • Participating as a member of a team • Acquiring and evaluating information • Organizing and maintaining information • Decision making • Reasoning	**1:** 0.1.2, 1.3.7 **2:** 1.2.1 **3:** 1.2.1, 1.2.2 **4:** 1.3.1 **5:** 1.2.5 **R:** 7.2.1 **TP:** 4.8.1., 4.8.5., 4.8.6.

Correlations to the latest state-specific standards are on our website.

Contents

CONTENTS

• Grammar points that are explicitly taught　　◇ Grammar points that are presented in context　　△ Grammar points that are being recycled

	Numeracy/ Academic Skills	EFF	SCANS	CASAS
Unit 3	• Pronunciation: Rising and falling intonation • Scanning • Active reading • Focused listening • Reading a bar graph • Budget arithmetic • Writing a business letter • Reviewing	Most EFF skills are incorporated into this unit with an emphasis on: • Learning through research • Reading with understanding • Conveying ideas in writing • Solving problems and making decisions (Technology is optional.)	Many SCAN skills are incorporated in this unit with an emphasis on: • Allocating money • Understanding systems • Monitoring and correcting performance • Interpreting and communicating information • Reading • Writing • Decision making	**1:** 1.4.1, 1.4.2 **2:** 1.4.2, 7.2.7 **3:** 1.4.4, 1.5.3 **4:** 1.5.1, 6.0.3, 6.0l.5, 6.1.1, 6.1.2 **5:** 1.4.7 **R:** 7.2.1 **TP:** 4.8.1, 4.8.5, 4.8.6.
Unit 4	• Pronunciation: Rising and falling intonation • Pronunciation: Phrasing • Focused listening • Making inferences • Reading charts • Reading a map • Paragraph writing • Reviewing	Most EFF skills are incorporated into this unit with an emphasis on: • Learning through research • Conveying ideas in writing • Solving problems and making decisions (Technology is optional.)	Many SCAN skills are incorporated in this unit with an emphasis on: • Understanding systems • Interpreting and communicating information • Writing • Decision making • Seeing things in the mind's eye	**1:** 0.1.2 **2:** 1.8.5, 2.5.6 **3:** 2.2.1, 2.2.5 **4:** 7.2.6 **5:** 7.2.2 **R:** 7.2.1 **TP:** 4.8.1, 4.8.5, 4.8.6
Unit 5	• Active listening • Active reading • Reviewing	Most EFF skills are incorporated into this unit with an emphasis on: • Reflecting and evaluating • Learning through research • Reading with understanding • Speaking so others can understand (Technology is optional.)	Many SCAN skills are incorporated in this unit with an emphasis on: • Understanding systems • Self management • Acquiring and evaluating information • Interpreting and communicating information	**1:** 3.1.1, 3.1.3, 3.2.1 **2:** 3.1.1 **3:** 3.4.2, 3.5.9 **4:** 3.5.1, 3.5.3, 3.5.5 3.5.9, 6.7.3 **5:** 3.5.9 **R:** 7.2.1 **TP:** 4.8.1, 4.8.5, 4.8.6.

CONTENTS

● Grammar points that are explicitly taught   ◊ Grammar points that are presented in context   △ Grammar points that are being recycled

Welcome to Stand Out, Second Edition

Stand Out works.

And now it works even better!

Built from the standards necessary for adult English learners, the second edition of *Stand Out* gives students the foundation and tools they need to develop confidence and become independent, lifelong learners.

- **Grammar** Charts clearly explain grammar points, and are followed by personalized exercises.
- **Pronunciation** activities are integrated through the program.

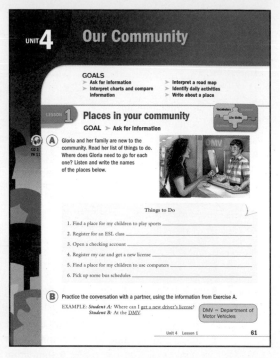

- Clearly defined **goals** provide a roadmap of learning for the student.
- Key **vocabulary** is introduced visually and orally.

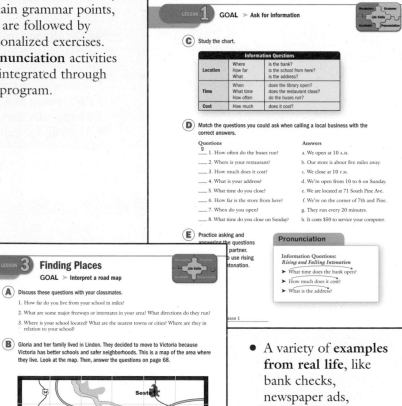

- A variety of **examples from real life**, like bank checks, newspaper ads, maps, etc. help students learn to access information and resources in their community.

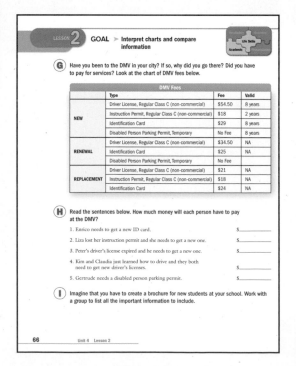

- State and federally required **life skills and competencies** are taught, helping students meet necessary benchmarks.

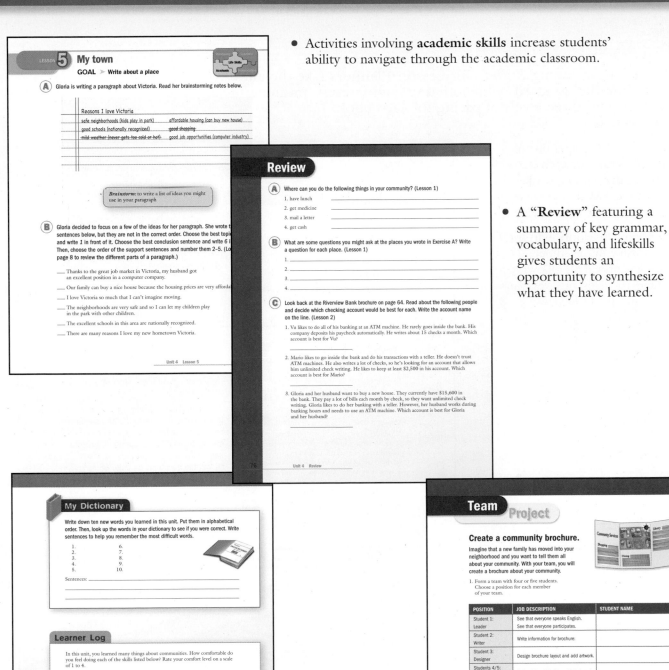

- Activities involving **academic skills** increase students' ability to navigate through the academic classroom.

- A **"Review"** featuring a summary of key grammar, vocabulary, and lifeskills gives students an opportunity to synthesize what they have learned.

- **"My Dictionary"** activity allows learners to use the vocabulary from the unit in a new way, increasing the likelihood that they will acquire the words.
- **"Learner Log"** provides opportunities for learner self-assessment.

- **"Team Projects"** present motivating cross-ability activities which group learners of different levels together to complete a task that applies the unit objective.

The ground-breaking *Stand Out* **Lesson Planners** take the guesswork out of meeting the standards while offering high-interest, meaningful language activities, and three levels of pacing for each book.

- An at-a-glance **agenda** and **prep section** for each lesson ensure that instructors have a clear knowledge of what will be covered in the lesson.

- A complete **lesson plan** for each page in the student book is provided, following a standard lesson progression (Warm-up and Review, Introduction, Presentation, Practice, Evaluation, and Application).

- Clear, easy-to-identify **pacing guide** icons offer three different pacing strategies.

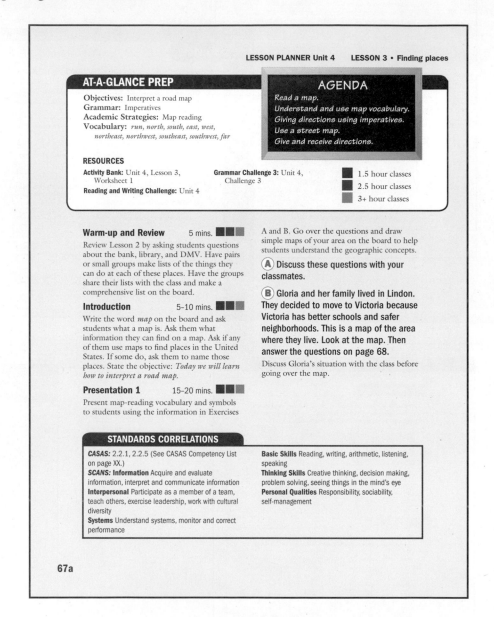

- "**Teaching Tips**" provide ideas and strategies for the classroom.
- Additional **supplemental activities** found on the *Activity Bank CD-ROM* are suggested at their point of use.
- The *Activity Bank CD-ROM* includes **reproducible multilevel activity masters** for each lesson that can be printed or downloaded and modified for classroom needs.
- "**Listening Scripts**" from the *Audio CD* are included.
- "**Standards Correlations**" appear directly on the page, detailing how *Stand Out* meets CASAS and SCANS standards.

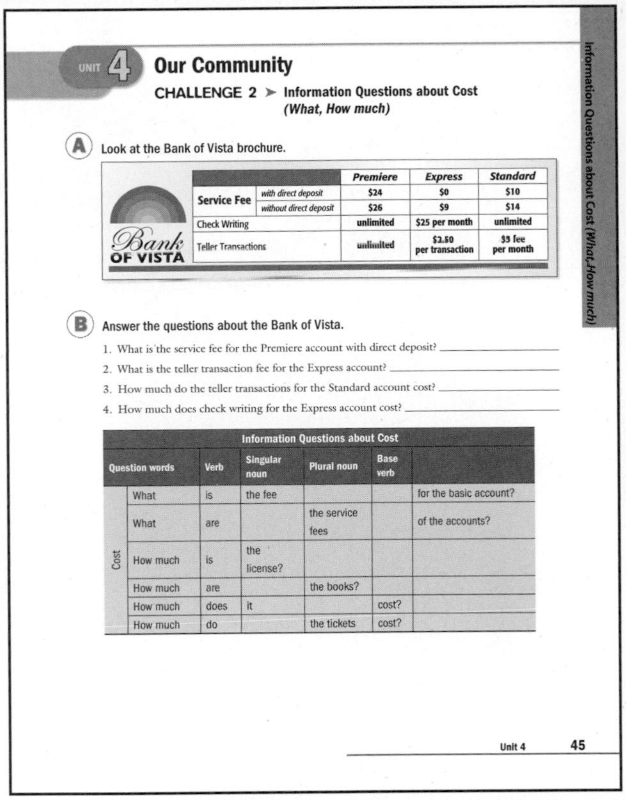

Information Questions about Cost (What, How much)

UNIT 4 **Our Community**

CHALLENGE 2 ➤ **Information Questions about Cost** ***(What, How much)***

A Look at the Bank of Vista brochure.

Bank OF VISTA

		Premiere	Express	Standard
Service Fee	with direct deposit	$24	$0	$10
	without direct deposit	$26	$9	$14
Check Writing		unlimited	$25 per month	unlimited
Teller Transactions		unlimited	$2.50 per transaction	$3 fee per month

B Answer the questions about the Bank of Vista.

1. What is the service fee for the Premiere account with direct deposit? ______
2. What is the teller transaction fee for the Express account? ______
3. How much do the teller transactions for the Standard account cost? ______
4. How much does check writing for the Express account cost? ______

Information Questions about Cost						
Question words		Verb	Singular noun	Plural noun	Base verb	
Cost	What	is	the fee			for the basic account?
	What	are		the service fees		of the accounts?
	How much	is	the license?			
	How much	are		the books?		
	How much	does	it		cost?	
	How much	do		the tickets	cost?	

Unit 4 45

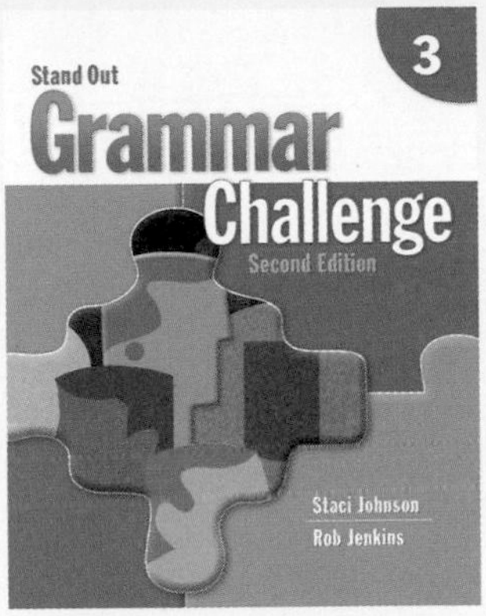

- ***Grammar Challenge*** workbooks include supplemental activities for students who desire even more contextual grammar and vocabulary practice.
- Clear and concise **grammar explanation boxes** provide a strong foundation for the activities.

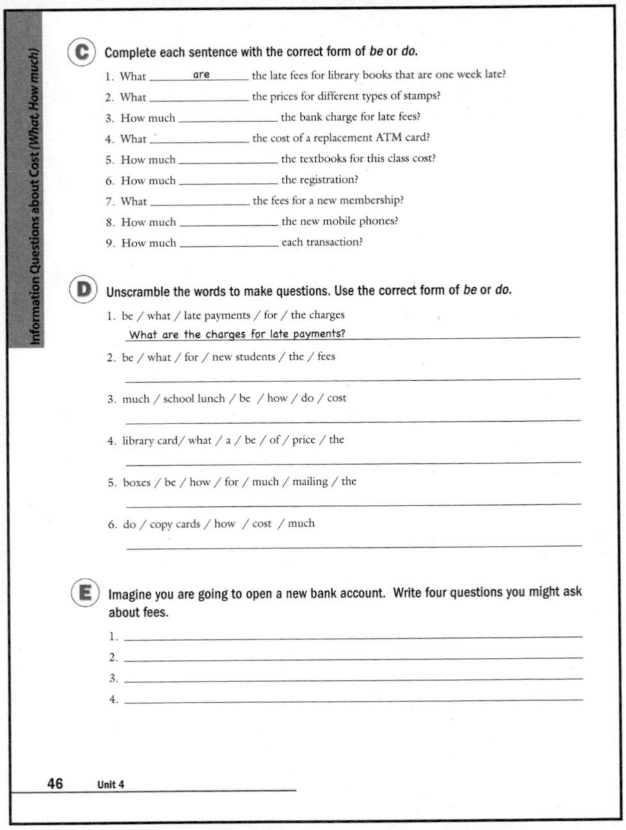

Information Questions about Cost (What, How much)

C Complete each sentence with the correct form of *be* or *do*.

1. What ___are___ the late fees for library books that are one week late?
2. What ______ the prices for different types of stamps?
3. How much ______ the bank charge for late fees?
4. What ______ the cost of a replacement ATM card?
5. How much ______ the textbooks for this class cost?
6. How much ______ the registration?
7. What ______ the fees for a new membership?
8. How much ______ the new mobile phones?
9. How much ______ each transaction?

D Unscramble the words to make questions. Use the correct form of *be* or *do*.

1. be / what / late payments / for / the charges
   What are the charges for late payments?
2. be / what / for / new students / the / fees
   ______
3. much / school lunch / be / how / do / cost
   ______
4. library card/ what / a / be / of / price / the
   ______
5. boxes / be / how / for / much / mailing / the
   ______
6. do / copy cards / how / cost / much
   ______

E Imagine you are going to open a new bank account. Write four questions you might ask about fees.

1. ______
2. ______
3. ______
4. ______

46 Unit 4

- A variety of **activities** allow students develop their grammar skills and apply them.
- Written by **Rob Jenkins** and **Staci Johnson**, the *Grammar Challenge* workbooks are directly aligned to the student books.

- ***Reading & Writing Challenge*** workbooks are also available. These workbooks provide challenging materials and exercises for students who want even more practice in reading, vocabulary development, and writing.

Getting to Know You

GOALS
➤ Introduce yourself and greet your friends
➤ Write about yourself
➤ Identify educational goals

LESSON **1**

Nice to meet you!

GOAL ➤ Introduce yourself
and greet your friends

A Fill out the school registration form with your personal information.

☀ SANTA ANA ADULT SCHOOL
Registration Form

First Name _____ Middle Initial _____

Last Name _____

Address:
Number and Street _____

City _____ State _____ Zip _____

Phone:
Home _____ Cell _____

E-mail address _____

Date of birth (mm/dd/yy) __ / __ / __

Languages Spoken _____

Occupation _____

B Write questions for the information on the registration form.

Question	Student A	Student B
What is your first name?		

C Now interview two classmates. Use the questions you wrote in Exercise B. Fill in the chart above with their answers.

EXAMPLE: *You:* What is your first name?
Student A: My first name is Michel.
You: What's your first name?
Student B: My first name is Selma.

Contractions
What is = *What's*
What's your name?

D Introduce the two classmates you interviewed to the rest of the class.

EXAMPLE: This is Michel. His last name is Caron. He is from Haiti. This is Selma. Her last name is Bezerra. She is from Brazil.

E Juan and Michel take English class together. Read their conversation.

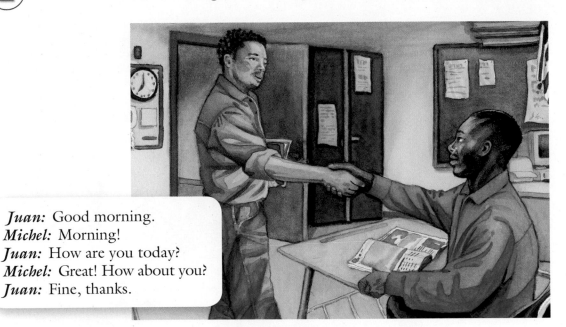

Juan: Good morning.
Michel: Morning!
Juan: How are you today?
Michel: Great! How about you?
Juan: Fine, thanks.

F Practice the conversation above with a partner.

 G Listen to the greetings and responses.

CD 1
TR 1

Greetings	Responses
Hi!	Hello!
Good morning!	Morning!
How are you today?	Fine. / Great!
How's it going?	Pretty good.
How are you doing?	OK. / Not bad.
What's up?	Nothing.
What's new?	Not much.

 H Now listen to the greetings and respond after each one.

CD 1
TR 2

I Greet three different classmates. Ask them a few personal information questions.

Tell your story.

GOAL ➤ Write about yourself

A Read about Akiko.

My name is Akiko Sugiyama and I'm a student at Santa Ana Adult School. I came to the United States five years ago from Japan with my husband and three children. We live in Santa Ana, California. My husband works in a computer assembly factory. I go to school and take care of our children. We are all studying English because we want to be successful in this country. Someday we hope to buy a house and send our children to college.

B Answer the questions about Akiko.

1. When did Akiko come to the United States? _____

2. Where is she from? _____

3. Who did she come to the United States with? _____

4. Where does she live? _____

5. What does her husband do? _____

6. What does she do? _____

7. Why is she studying English? _____

8. What are her future goals? _____

GOAL ➤ **Write about yourself**

C **Now answer the questions about yourself.**

1. When did you come to this country? _____

2. Where are you from? _____

3. Who did you come to this country with? _____

4. Where do you live? _____

5. What do you do? _____

6. Why are you studying English? _____

7. What are your future goals? _____

D **Study the paragraph below. Notice the title, the margins, and the indented first line.**

title

space between title and paragraph

My Story

indent

My name is Akiko Sugiyama and I'm a student at Santa Ana Adult School. I came to the United States five years ago from Japan with my husband and three children. We live in Santa Ana, California. My husband works in a computer assembly factory. I go to school and take care of our children. We are all studying English because we want to be successful in this country. Someday we hope to buy a house and send our children to college.

right margin

left margin

GOAL ➤ **Write about yourself**

Vocabulary   Grammar
Life Skills
Academic   Pronunciation

E Write a paragraph about yourself with the answers you wrote in Exercise C. Use correct paragraph formatting like Akiko's paragraph in Exercise D.

 F Show your paragraph to your partner. Read your partner's paragraph and ask questions about anything you want to know more about.

Are you college bound?

GOAL ➤ **Identify educational goals**

A This pyramid represents the educational system in the United States. Read the pyramid with your teacher.

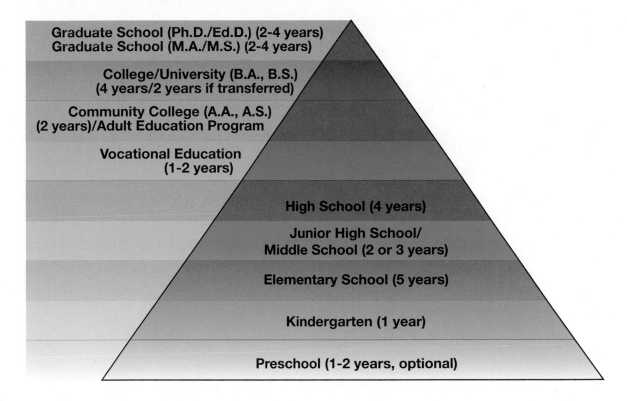

Graduate School (Ph.D./Ed.D.) (2-4 years)
Graduate School (M.A./M.S.) (2-4 years)

College/University (B.A., B.S.)
(4 years/2 years if transferred)

Community College (A.A., A.S.)
(2 years)/Adult Education Program

Vocational Education
(1-2 years)

High School (4 years)

Junior High School/
Middle School (2 or 3 years)

Elementary School (5 years)

Kindergarten (1 year)

Preschool (1-2 years, optional)

B What do these abbreviations stand for and mean? Have your teacher help you complete the chart.

Abbreviation	Stands for . . .	Meaning
A.A.	Associate of Arts	a two-year degree from a community college with an art-related major
A.S.		
M.A.		
M.S.		
Ph.D.		
Ed.D.		

 Choose the best answer. Look back at the pyramid if you need help.

1. What is the lowest level of education in the United States?

   a. kindergarten   b. preschool   c. graduate school

2. How many years do students go to high school?

   a. three years   b. two years   c. four years

3. What is the highest degree you can get?

   a. M.A.   b. M.S.   c. Ph.D.

4. Where can you get a B.A. or B.S. degree?

   a. college   b. graduate school   c. technical college

D How is the U.S. educational system different from the educational system in your country? Use the pyramid below to show your country's educational system. Then, compare pyramids with a classmate.

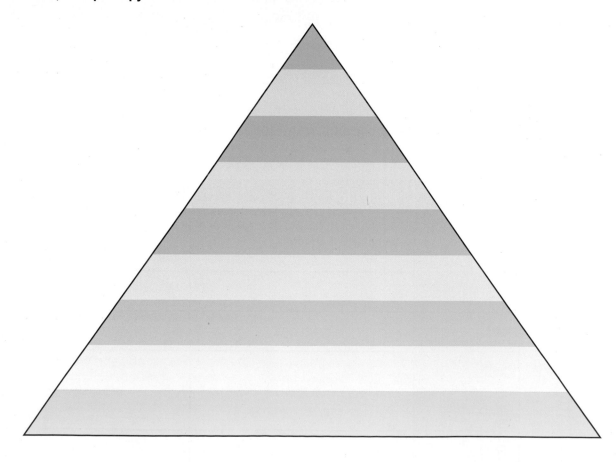

E Where are you on the educational pyramid?

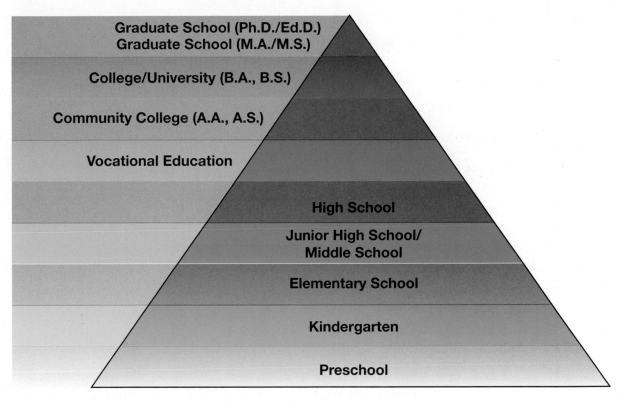

Graduate School (Ph.D./Ed.D.)
Graduate School (M.A./M.S.)
College/University (B.A., B.S.)
Community College (A.A., A.S.)
Vocational Education
High School
Junior High School/
Middle School
Elementary School
Kindergarten
Preschool

1. Put a check (✓) on the pyramid next to the educational levels you have completed (in any country).

2. Where do you want to be? Circle the educational level that you would like to achieve.

F How do you plan to achieve your educational goals? Write a short paragraph.

_____

_____

_____

_____

_____

My Dictionary

Find three new words you learned in this unit. Write the word and the sentence where you found the word.

EXAMPLE: Word: future   Page: P5
            Sentence: What are her <u>future</u> goals?

1. Word: _____   Page: ____

   Sentence: _____

2. Word: _____   Page: ____

   Sentence: _____

3. Word: _____   Page: ____

   Sentence: _____

Learner Log

In this unit, you had a chance to meet your classmates, share something about yourself, and think about your educational goals. How comfortable do you feel doing each of the skills listed below? Rate your comfort level on a scale of 1 to 4.

1 = Need more practice   **2** = OK   **3** = Good   **4** = Great!

Life Skill	Comfort Level				Page
I can fill out a registration form.	1	2	3	4	____
I can introduce myself.	1	2	3	4	____
I can greet my friends.	1	2	3	4	____
I can ask personal information questions.	1	2	3	4	____
I can write a paragraph.	1	2	3	4	____
I can write my educational goals.	1	2	3	4	____

If you circled 1 or 2, write down the page number where you can review this skill.

Reflection

1. What was the most useful skill you learned in this unit? _____

2. How will this help you in life? _____

Balancing Your Life

GOALS

➤ **Make a schedule**
➤ **Identify goals, obstacles, and solutions**
➤ **Write about your goal**

➤ **Identify study habits**
➤ **Identify time-management strategies**

 LESSON **1**

Everyday life

GOAL ➤ **Make a schedule**

Vocabulary — Grammar
Life Skills
Academic — Pronunciation

A Look at Luisa's schedule. What are her routines?

	Monday	Tuesday	Wednesday	Thursday	Friday	Saturday	Sunday
Morning 6-8 A.M.	Go running	Go to grocery store	Go running	Clean house	Breakfast with coworkers	Go running	
8-12 A.M./P.M.	Day off	Work 10:00	Work 10:00	Work 10:00	Work 10:00	Work 10:00	Day off
Afternoon 12-1 P.M.	Go shopping with Mary	Go to bank on lunch break				Go to library on lunch break	Have lunch with family
1-5 P.M.		Finish work 5:00	Finish work 5:00		Finish work 5:00	Finish work 5:00	
Evening 5-9 P.M.		ESL class 7-8	Computer class 6:30-7:30	Finish work 5:00	ESL class 7-8	Rent a video	

B Talk about Luisa's schedule with a partner. Ask questions using: *What time . . . ?, When . . . ?,* and *What . . . ?*

EXAMPLE: *Student A:* What time does Luisa start work?
Student B: She starts work at 10:00 A.M.

LESSON 1   **GOAL** ➤ **Make a schedule**

C With a partner, ask questions about Luisa's schedule. Use *How often . . . ?* Answer the questions using the frequency expressions from the box.

once a week	twice a week	three times a week
every morning	every weekday	every other day every Saturday

EXAMPLE: *Student A:* How often does Luisa rent a movie?
                    Student B: Luisa rents a movie every Saturday.

D Where do these adverbs of frequency go in a sentence? Study the charts below.

0%   50%   100%

never   rarely   sometimes   usually   always

Placement rules for frequency adverbs	Examples
before the main verb	Luisa *always / usually / often* <u>goes</u> running. She *sometimes / rarely / never* <u>makes</u> dinner.
after the main verb *be*	She <u>is</u> *usually* busy on the weekends.
sometimes / usually / often can come at the beginning or at the end of a sentence	*Usually / Sometimes* Luisa studies in the library. Luisa studies in the library *sometimes / usually.*
between the subject and verb in short answers	Yes, <u>I</u> *always* <u>do</u>. / No, <u>he</u> *usually* <u>isn't</u>.
Rarely and *never* are negative words. Do not use *not* and *never* in the same sentence.	**Correct:** He *never* goes to the movies. **Incorrect:** He ~~doesn't~~ never go to the movies.

E Write the frequency adverb in parentheses in the correct place in each sentence below. Remember, sometimes the adverb can go in more than one place.

                          rarely
EXAMPLE: Roberto ᐯ finishes his homework before class. (rarely)

1. Jerry comes to class on time. (always)

2. Sue eats lunch with her husband. (sometimes)

3. Our teacher sits at her desk while she is teaching. (never)

4. Hugo works at night. (usually)

2   Unit 1   Lesson 1

F Write sentences about Luisa, using frequency adverbs. Look back at her schedule on page 1.

EXAMPLE: Luisa usually finishes work at 5:00.

1. _____

2. _____

3. _____

4. _____

G Practice reading the sentences you wrote in Exercise F. Focus on the important words.

Pronunciation

Focus: In a phrase or sentence, certain words get the most stress or *focus*. In the sentences below, the words with the most focus are in CAPITAL letters.

Luisa OFTEN goes RUNNING.

She is NEVER HOME on the weekends.

SOMETIMES I go to the MOVIES.

He RARELY studies in the MORNING.

H Make a schedule of everything you do in one week. Talk about your schedule with your partner.

EXAMPLE: I NEVER cook on my day off because I'm a cook in a restaurant!

	Monday	Tuesday	Wednesday	Thursday	Friday	Saturday	Sunday
Morning							
Afternoon							
Evening							

The future

GOAL ➤ Identify goals, obstacles, and solutions

Zhou is worried about the future. What is he thinking about?

A Read about Zhou.

Zhou's life is going to change very soon. His wife, Huixen, is going to have twins in July. His parents are going to come from China to live in the United States. He's happy, but his apartment will to be too small for everyone. He needs a better job, but his boss won't promote him because he doesn't have a college degree.

Zhou has three goals. When his parents come to the United States, he will buy a house large enough for two families. His father will work and help pay for the house. His mother will help take care of the children. Then, Zhou plans to go to night school and get his bachelor's degree. When he graduates, he will apply for a new position at work. He will work hard to achieve his goals.

B A *goal* is something you would like to achieve in the future. What are Zhou's three goals?

Contractions
will not = *won't*
His boss *won't* promote him.

1. _____

2. _____

3. _____

 C An *obstacle* is a problem, or something that gets in the way of your goal. Zhou has two obstacles. What are they?

1. _____

2. _____

GOAL ➤ Identify goals, obstacles, and solutions

Vocabulary   Grammar
Life Skills
Academic   Pronunciation

D **Review vocabulary.**

1. What is a goal? _____

2. What is an obstacle? _____

3. What is a solution? <u>A solution is an idea of how to solve a problem.</u>

4. Zhou's apartment is too small. What is his solution?

_____

5. Zhou needs a better job. What is his solution?

_____

 E **Listen to Tuba and Lam. Identify their goals, obstacles, and solutions and write them in the spaces below.**

CD 1
TR 3

1. **Goal:** Tuba wants to <u>get a job to help her husband</u> .

   Obstacle: Her obstacle is _____ .

   Solutions: _____

A. Maybe she can _____ .

B. Maybe her mother can _____ .

2. **Goal:** Lam wants to _____ .

   Obstacle: His obstacle is _____ .

   Solutions: _____

A. Maybe his grandchildren can _____ .

B. Maybe his grandchildren can _____ .

F **Look at how we can talk about Zhou's goals.**

When Zhou *graduates*, he *will* apply for a new position at work.
This sentence means:
First, he will graduate. *Then*, he will apply for a new position at work.

When his parents *come* to the United States, he *will* buy a house.
This sentence means:
First, his parents will come to the United States. *Then*, he will buy a house.

Future Time Clauses with *When*

When	Present tense	*Will*	Base verb
When Zhou	graduates,	he will	apply for a new position at work.*
When his parents	come to the United States	he will	buy a house.

*Note: The order of the clauses does not matter. You can also say, *Zhou will apply for a new position at work when he graduates.*

G   Complete the sentences below with your own ideas.

EXAMPLE: When his parents come to the United States, <u>Zhou's house</u>

<u>will be too small</u>.

1. When _____, they will buy a bigger house.

2. When Zhou's mother comes to stay, _____.

3. When _____, his boss will promote him.

4. When Zhou gets a better job, _____.

H   Look back at Zhou's goals. He has a *personal* goal (buy a new home), an *educational* goal (graduate from college), and an *occupational* goal (get a new position at work). What are your goals? Write them in the chart below.

Personal	Educational	Occupational
<u>run a 5k race</u>	<u>take an English course</u>	<u>get a raise at work</u>
1. _____	1. _____	1. _____
2. _____	2. _____	2. _____
3. _____	3. _____	3. _____

I   In groups, discuss your goals for the future. Then, write sentences about yourself.

EXAMPLE: <u>When I graduate, I will get a new job.</u>

J   **Active Task.** Write or type your goals on a piece of paper. Hang it up in a special place where you can read your goals each day.

Goals, obstacles, and solutions

GOAL ➤ Write about your goal

A Read the paragraph and review the meanings of the words in italics.

In the previous lesson, you wrote your *goals*. Goals are things you want to *achieve*. Sometimes we can have *problems* achieving our goals. These problems are called *obstacles*. When we figure out how to *solve* these problems, we have *solutions*.

B Choose one of the goals you wrote in the chart on page 6. Think of one obstacle to reaching your goal and two possible solutions. Write the information below.

Goal: _____

Obstacle: _____

Solutions:

1. _____

   _____

2. _____

   _____

C Share your ideas with a partner. Can your partner suggest other possible solutions?

Solutions from my partner:

_____

_____

_____

_____

GOAL ➤ **Write about your goal**

D What is a paragraph? Discuss the following terms with your teacher.

➤ A *paragraph* is a group of sentences about the same topic.

➤ A *topic sentence* is usually the first sentence in a paragraph and it introduces the topic or *main idea*.

➤ *Support sentences* are the sentences that follow the topic sentence. They give *details* about the topic.

➤ A *conclusion sentence* is the final sentence of the paragraph. It gives a *summary* of the paragraph.

E In Lesson 2, you heard Tuba talk about her goal. Now, read about her goal. Study the paragraph with your teacher.

indent · topic sentence · **My Goal** · title

My goal is to get a job to help my husband with money. I have an obstacle—time. It will be difficult to work because I have to take care of the children and the house. One solution is to work part-time while my children are in school. Another solution is to have my mother help take care of the children. If we all work together, we will achieve our goal.

support sentences

conclusion sentence

LESSON 3 **GOAL** ➤ **Write about your goal**

Vocabulary   Grammar
Life Skills
Academic   Pronunciation

F Answer the questions about Tuba's paragraph. Then, write ideas for your own paragraph about the goal you chose on page 7.

1. What is Tuba's topic sentence?

_____

_____

2. Tuba's support sentences are about her obstacle and her two possible solutions. What are her support sentences?

_____

_____

_____

3. What is Tuba's conclusion sentence?

_____

_____

1. Write your topic sentence.

_____

_____

2. Write your three support sentences.

A. _____

B. _____

C. _____

3. Write your conclusion sentence.

_____

_____

G Write a paragraph about your goal using correct paragraph formatting. Make sure your first sentence is a topic sentence. Follow your topic sentence with support sentences. Write a conclusion sentence at the end of your paragraph.

_____

_____

_____

_____

_____

_____

_____

GOAL ➤ Identify study habits

A Write answers to the following questions. Then, compare your answers with a partner.

1. Where do you like to study? _____

2. When do you usually study? _____

3. How long do you study? _____

4. Do you listen to music when you study? Why or why not? _____

_____

B Look at the first picture. What is Luisa doing? Do you think she is learning anything? Why or why not? Look at the second picture. What is Michel doing? Is he learning anything? Discuss your ideas with a partner.

Don't you have class at 7:00?

What page was I supposed to read?

Shhh it's 6:30. Dad is studying now.

 C Listen to the reading about study habits. Listen for good and bad study habits.

CD 1
TR 4

D Read the paragraphs about study habits below.

Good study habits can be very *beneficial* to you and your education. On the other hand, bad study habits can be *harmful* to your educational goals. First, let's talk about bad study habits.

Many people have very busy schedules and it is difficult for them to find time to study. One bad study habit is not studying before class. Another bad study habit is studying with *distractions* around, such as television, people talking, or loud music. A third bad study habit is copying a friend's homework. These are just a few bad study habits, but you can easily change them into good study habits.

There are many ways that you can improve your study habits. First, set a time every day to study and try to study at the same time every day. Do not make appointments at this time. This is your special study time. Second, find a good place to study, a place that is quiet and comfortable so you can *concentrate*. Finally, do your homework on your own. Afterwards, you can find a friend to help you *go over* your work and check your answers.

E According to the reading, what are some bad study habits? Write them below and add one more idea.

EXAMPLE: not studying before class _____

_____

_____

F According to the reading, what are some good study habits? Write them below and add one more idea.

EXAMPLE: studying at the same time every day _____

_____

_____

LESSON 4   **GOAL** ➤ **Identify study habits**

 G Match each vocabulary word or phrase with its correct definition.

1. _b_ improve   a. bad for you

2. ___ beneficial   b. get better

3. ___ harmful   c. review or check again

4. ___ distractions   d. good for you

5. ___ concentrate   e. think hard about something

6. ___ go over   f. things that disturb your study

H Fill in the blanks with a word or phrase from Exercise G.

1. My English will _____ if I practice every day.

2. Please be quiet. I can't _____ on my homework.

3. Studying with a friend can be _____ because you can help each other.

4. When you finish taking a test, _____ your answers again.

5. It's hard to study when there are _____. Turn off the TV!

6. Bad study habits can be _____ to your educational goals.

I Choose three words or phrases from Exercise G and write sentences about your study habits on a piece of paper. Share your sentences with a partner.

J Think about your study habits. Fill in the chart below.

Good study habits	Bad study habits
I study every day.	I watch the news and do my homework at the same time.
1.	1.
2.	2.
3.	3.

 K Share your answers with a partner. Which study habits are the same? Which study habits are different?

Time management

GOAL ➤ Identify time-management strategies

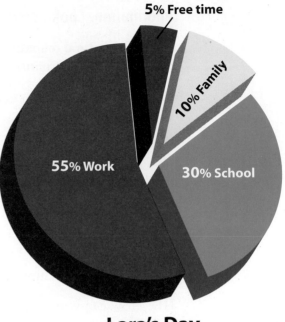

5% Free time

10% Family

55% Work

30% School

Lara's Day

A Read about Lara's problem.

Lara doesn't get to spend enough time with her family. The pie chart shows how Lara spends her time. As you can see, she rarely has any free time to relax. Lara wants to find a way to balance her time. So, she has decided to attend a lecture at school to learn better time-management strategies.

B Answer the questions about Lara.

1. What is Lara's goal?

_____

2. What is her obstacle?

_____

3. What is her solution?

_____

C Listen to the lecture about time management. Listen for the main ideas.

CD 1
TR 5

GOAL ➤ Identify time-management strategies

 D When you listen to a lecture, you can use an outline to help record important information. Look at the outline below and discuss it with your teacher.

I. Why is time management important?
   A. You stay organized.

   B. You accomplish everything that needs to get done.

   C. You _____.

II. How do you keep a schedule?
    A. Write down everything you need to do in a week.

    B. Put each task in a time slot.

    C. _____.

    D. Check off things that have been completed.

III. How can you add more time to your day?
     A. You can wake up earlier.

     B. You can ask _____.

     C. You can try doing _____ tasks at once.

IV. What are other important things to consider about time management?
    A. Remember the important people in your life.

    B. _____.

    C. You are the boss of your schedule.

V. What are the benefits of managing your time?
   A. You will have more time.

   B. You will feel less _____.

   C. You will have time to _____.

   D. You will feel better about yourself.

 E Listen to the lecture on time management again and complete the outline above.

CD 1
TR 5

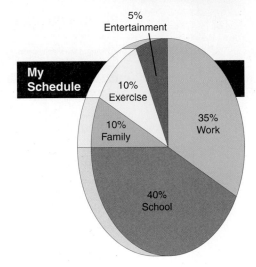

F A pie chart is a circle, like a pie, and is divided up into segments that equal 100%. From the pie chart on the right, fill in the percentages below and add them up. Do they equal 100%?

Work: _____ %
School: _____ %
Family: _____ %
Exercise: _____ %
Entertainment: _____ %
_____
TOTAL _____ %

G Fill in the pie chart on the right to show how you spend your time. Make sure your graph equals 100%!

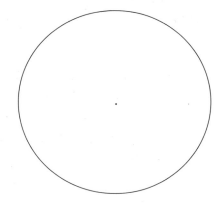

H Answer the following questions about your own time-management strategies.

1. What problems do you have with time?

EXAMPLE: <u>I work ten hours a day and I don't have time to study.</u>

_____

_____

2. How could you add more time to your day? (Think about what you learned from the lecture.)

_____

_____

3. What are some time-management skills you learned today that you would like to use

in your life? _____

_____

Review

A Exchange books with a partner. Have your partner complete the schedule below about himself or herself. (Lesson 1)

	Monday	Tuesday	Wednesday	Thursday	Friday	Saturday	Sunday
Morning							
Afternoon							
Evening							

B Write sentences about your partner's schedule using the frequency adverbs. (Lesson 1)

1. (always) _____

2. (usually) _____

3. (often) _____

4. (sometimes) _____

5. (rarely) _____

6. (never) _____

C Now share your sentences with your partner and see if he or she agrees.

EXAMPLE: *Student A:* You always work in the evenings.
  Student B: That's true.

D Complete the sentences with the correct verb form. (Lesson 2)

1. When Jason _____ (get) a better job, he _____ (buy) a new house.

2. Lilia _____ (join) her sister at college when she _____ (finish) her ESL class.

3. We _____ (run) a marathon when we _____ (complete) our training program.

4. When Maria _____ (get) her bachelor's degree, she

_____ (ask) her boss for a raise.

E What are your goals for the future? Write four sentences about your future goals using *when*. (Lesson 2)

EXAMPLE: <u>When I finish this course, I will take the GED exam.</u>

1. _____

2. _____

3. _____

4. _____

F Think of one obstacle and one solution for each goal you wrote in Exercise E. Complete the chart. (Lessons 2 and 3)

	Goal	Obstacle	Solution
1.			
2.			
3.			
4.			

G Match each word or phrase to its correct meaning. Draw a line. (Lesson 3)

1. paragraph   a. introduces your topic, or main idea

2. topic sentence   b. give details about your topic

3. support sentences   c. gives a summary of everything you wrote

4. conclusion sentence d. a group of sentences about the same topic

Review

H Read the following sentences that make up a paragraph. Label each as a *topic* sentence (T), a *support* sentence (S), or a *conclusion* sentence (C). Remember, there can only be one topic sentence and one conclusion sentence. (Lesson 3)

1. I will buy books to study with and I will study very hard. ___

2. Within the next two years, I hope to have my license. ___

3. When I'm ready, I will register for the test. ___

4. My goal for the future is to get my real estate license. ___

5. When I am close to taking the test, I will ask my friend, who is a realtor,

   to help me. ___

I On a piece of paper, rewrite the sentences above in the correct order, using correct paragraph formatting. (Lesson 3)

J Write two good study habits. (Lesson 4)

   1. _____

   2. _____

K Write two good time-management strategies. (Lesson 5)

   1. _____

   2. _____

L Write the correct word from the box for each definition. (Lessons 2–4)

beneficial	concentrate	distractions	go over
goal	harmful	improve	obstacle

1. bad for you _____

2. when you get better at something _____

3. good for you _____

4. think hard about something _____

5. something you want to achieve _____

6. a problem _____

7. review something or check it again _____

8. things that bother you when you are studying _____

My Dictionary

Choose three words from this unit. Write the new words and a definition for each one in your vocabulary notebook. Draw pictures to help you remember the new words.

EXAMPLES:

Goal - something I want to achieve

GOAL

Obstacle - something that stops you from getting to your goal

Solution - a way to overcome the problem

Learner Log

In this unit, you learned many things about balancing your life. How comfortable do you feel doing each of the skills listed below? Rate your comfort level on a scale of 1 to 4.

1 = Need more practice   **2** = OK   **3** = Good   **4** = Great!

Life Skill	Comfort Level				Page
I can make a schedule.	1	2	3	4	_____
I can identify my future goals, obstacles, and solutions.	1	2	3	4	_____
I can write about my goals.	1	2	3	4	_____
I know how to improve study habits.	1	2	3	4	_____
I can use good time-managment strategies.	1	2	3	4	_____
I can listen to a lecture and use an outline.	1	2	3	4	_____

If you circled 1 or 2, write down the page number where you can review this skill.

Reflection

1. What was the most useful skill you learned in this unit? _____

2. How will this help you in life? _____

Team Project

Make a schedule.

With a team, you will design a weekly schedule that includes your class and study time. You will identify good study habits and time-management strategies that you will use during this class.

1. Form a team with four or five students. Choose a position for each member of your team.

POSITION	JOB DESCRIPTION	STUDENT NAME
Student 1: Leader	See that everyone speaks English and participates.	
Student 2: Secretary	Take notes on study habits and time-management strategies.	
Student 3: Designer	Design a weekly schedule.	
Students 4/5: Assistants	Help the secretary and the designer with their work.	

2. Design a weekly schedule. On your schedule, write in the days and times you have English class. (Lesson 1)

3. Decide on a goal that is related to learning English. Think of one obstacle to your goal. Think of two solutions. (Lessons 2–3)

4. Make a list of good study habits and a list of time-management strategies you'd like to use. (Lessons 4–5)

5. Make a poster with all of the information from above: weekly schedule, goal, obstacle, solutions, good study habits, and time-management strategies.

6. Present your poster to the class.

UNIT 2

Consumer Smarts

GOALS

➤ Identify places to purchase goods and services

➤ Interpret advertisements

➤ Compare products

➤ Identify and compare purchasing methods

➤ Make a smart purchase

LESSON 1 Shopping for goods and services

GOAL ➤ Identify places to purchase goods and services

A What kind of stores or businesses are these? What goods or services can you purchase here?

B Look at the places below. Which of them sell goods? Which of them provide services?

laundromat	gas station	pharmacy	hotel
jewelry store	bank	post office	department store
grocery store	car wash	tailors	office supply store
drugstore	dry cleaners	hardware store	hair salon

Unit 2   Lesson 1   21

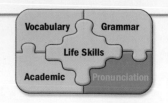

LESSON **1**   **GOAL** ➤ Identify places to purchase goods and services

C Fill in the chart using the places from Exercise B. Then, add two places of your own to each list.

Sells goods	Provides services	Both
grocery store	laundromat	post office

D Where can you purchase each of the following items? Write the places. Some items may have more than one answer.

Item	Place
1. medicine	pharmacy
2. a table	
3. a notebook	
4. a bracelet	
5. boots	
6. a refrigerator	
7. bread	
8. motor oil	
9. a shirt	
10. stamps	

E We use the expression *to get something done* when we talk about services we receive. Study the chart with your teacher.

to get something done				
Subject	**get**	**Object**	**Past participle**	**Example sentence**
I	get	my hair	cut	I get my hair cut every month. (present)
she	got	her clothes	cleaned	She got her clothes cleaned yesterday. (past)
For a list of past participles, see p. 163 in the back of this book.				

GOAL ➤ Identify places to purchase goods and services

F Where can you receive the following services? Write the places on the lines. Some items may have more than one answer.

EXAMPLE: get your clothes cleaned __dry cleaners__

1. get your hair cut _____
2. get your checks cashed _____
3. get your pants hemmed _____
4. get your car washed _____
5. get your car fixed _____
6. get your clothes washed _____

G Answer the following questions with complete sentences.

EXAMPLE: Where do you get your clothes cleaned?
__I get my clothes cleaned at the dry cleaners.__

1. Where do you get your hair cut?

_____

2. Where did you get your prescription filled?

_____

3. Where do you get your packages mailed?

_____

4. Where did you get your keys made?

_____

5. Where did you get your gas tank filled up?

_____

6. Where do you get your clothes washed?

_____

 H Imagine you are new to the neighborhood. Ask your partner questions about businesses in the area.

EXAMPLE: *Student A:* Where can I get my car washed?
  Student B: at the car wash on Maple Street

 Active Task. Go to a mall and look at the directory. What different stores and businesses does it have? Make a list to share with your class.

Advertisements

GOAL ➤ Interpret advertisements

 A Write answers to the following questions. Then, discuss your answers with your classmates.

1. What are advertisements? _____

2. Where can you find them? _____

3. What information can you find in advertisements? Make a list. _____

_____

 B Read the advertisements from the newspaper.

1.
BOB'S AUTO SERVICE
- Save on oil change
- Most cars now **only $16.95**
- Includes up to five quarts of oil, new oil filter, and labor
- Not valid with any other offer
- Offer expires 8/5/2009

2.
16 x 7 garage doors
McKINNON'S Garage Door Sale
Includes: delivery and installation of new door, 3-year warranty

Call now for your free in home estimate
1-800-555-3936

only $599.00

licensed and insured
exp. 2-21-2009

3.
★ STEREO ★ ★ FACTORY ★ ★ OUTLET ★
30-70% off original prices

Headphones   Speakers

starting at $9.95   starting at $79.95 a pair

$5 DISCOUNT WITH THIS AD

4.

All mountain bikes on sale!
Wheel World Bike Sale

SAVE 25%

All bikes come with 1-year warranty
Bikes reg. priced $150 now $112.50

C Read the ads again and find words with these meanings.

1. discount _____on sale_____   5. no charge _____

2. guarantee _____   6. approximate cost _____

3. work _____   7. to set up for use _____

4. to come to an end _____   8. normal _____

GOAL ➤ Interpret advertisements

D Read the ads again and bubble in the circle next to the correct answer.

1. What does the oil change NOT include?

○ oil   ○ oil filter   ○ windshield-wiper fluid

2. When does the offer expire for the oil change?

○ May 8, 2009   ○ August 8, 2009   ○ August 5, 2009

3. When does the garage door offer end?

○ February 21, 2009   ○ December 2, 2009   ○ February 2, 2009

4. What does the garage door purchase NOT include?

○ new door installation   ○ removal of old door   ○ three-year warranty

5. How do you get an in-home estimate for a new garage door?

○ call   ○ go to the company   ○ write a letter

6. What is for sale at the stereo factory outlet?

○ stereo speakers   ○ headphones   ○ stereo speakers and headphones

7. What is the discount at the outlet?

○ $9.95   ○ 30-70 percent   ○ $79.95

8. What is the regular price of the bikes?

○ $150.00   ○ $112.99   ○ $250.00

9. How much are the bikes discounted?

○ $25   ○ 25%   ○ $37.00

10. Which item(s) come with a warranty?

○ garage doors   ○ bicycles   ○ garage doors and bicycles

E Which ad do you like the best?

_____

Why?_____

_____

GOAL ➤ Interpret advertisements

F Read the two ads and complete the table below.

Cleaning Services		
Company		
Phone Number		
Product or Service		
Price		
Discounts		
Other Information		

Which cleaning service would you choose? _____

Why?_____

_____

G In groups, choose a product or service and create an advertisement for it. Include the name of your company, the name of your product, a small picture or illustration, and details of prices and discounts.

H **Active Task.** Find some newspaper advertisements and bring them to class. What special offers can you find?

Making Comparisons

GOAL ➤ **Compare products**

A Think about the different parts of a computer. What do you use them for?
Use the words from the box to label the picture.

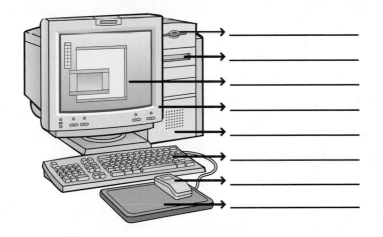

_____

_____

_____

_____

_____

_____

_____

monitor	CD-ROM drive
mouse	keyboard
screen	CPU
mousepad	hard drive

B What should you look for when you buy a computer?

Speed: Is the computer *fast* or *slow*?
Monitor: Is the screen *large* or *small*?
Memory: How *much* memory does the computer have?
Price: Is the computer *expensive* or *cheap*?
Hard Drive: Is the hard drive *big* or *small*?

GHz = gigahertz
1,000 MHz = 1 GHz
MB = megabytes
GB = gigabytes
1,000 MB = 1 GB
15" = 15 inches

C Study the information about five different computers. Use the adjectives above to talk about them.

EXAMPLE: The JCN computer has a large monitor.

	JCN	Doshiba	Vintel	Shepland	Kontaq
Price	$1,371	$1,549	$794	$1,168	$419
Speed	3.1 GHz	3.2 GHz	2.66 GHz	3.0 GHz	2.4 GHz
Monitor Size	20"	20"	22"	17"	17"
Memory	2 GB	3 GB	512 MB	1 GB	256 MB
Hard Drive	160 GB	250 GB	80 GB	160 GB	80 GB

D   Study the chart with your classmates and teacher.

Comparatives				
	Adjective	**Comparative**	**Rule**	**Example sentence**
Short adjectives	cheap	cheaper	Add *-er* to the end of the adjective.	Your computer was *cheaper* than my computer.
Long adjectives	expensive	more expensive	Add *more* before the adjective.	The new computer was *more expensive* than the old one.
Irregular adjectives	good / bad	better / worse	These adjectives are irregular.	The computer at school is *better* than this one.
Remember to use *than* after a comparative adjective followed by a noun.				

E   Use the rules above to make comparative adjectives.

1. slow   <u>slower</u>   5. heavy   _____

2. small   _____   6. fast   _____

3. wide   _____   7. beautiful   _____

4. big   _____   8. interesting   _____

Spelling
hot ⟶ **hotter**
easy ⟶ **easier**
large ⟶ **larger**
pretty ⟶ **prettier**

F   Make comparative sentences about the computers on page 27.

EXAMPLE: The Kontaq / slow / the Vintel   <u>The Kontaq is slower than the Vintel.</u>

1. The JCN monitor / wide / the Shepland monitor

_____

2. The Doshiba / fast / the Vintel

_____

3. The JCN's hard drive / big / the Kontaq

_____

G   Talk to your partner. Which computer from page 27 would you buy? Using comparatives, give three reasons for your choice.

GOAL ➤ **Compare products**

H Study the chart with your teacher.

Superlatives				
	Adjective	**Superlative**	**Rule**	**Example sentence**
Short adjectives	cheap	the cheapest	Add -*est* to the end of the adjective.	Your computer is *the cheapest*.
Long adjectives	expensive	the most expensive	Add *most* before the adjective.	He bought *the most* expensive computer in the store.
Irregular adjectives	good bad	best worst	These adjectives are irregular.	The computers at school are *the best*.
	Always use *the* before a superlative.			

I Use the rules above to make superlative adjectives.

Spelling	
hot	➜ the hottest
easy	➜ the easiest
large	➜ the largest
pretty	➜ the prettiest

1. slow   <u>the slowest</u>   5. heavy   _____

2. small   _____   6. fast   _____

3. wide   _____   7. beautiful   _____

4. big   _____   8. interesting   _____

J Make superlative sentences about the computers on page 27.

EXAMPLE: wide   <u>The Vintel computer has the widest screen.</u>

1. expensive   _____

2. cheap   _____

3. slow   _____

4. large memory   _____

5. small memory   _____

K Write six questions about the computers on page 27, using comparatives and superlatives. Walk around the room and ask your classmates to answer your questions.

EXAMPLE: Which computer has the biggest monitor?
                Which computer is faster, the JCN or the Doshiba?

LESSON **4** **Cash or charge?**

GOAL ➤ **Identify and compare purchasing methods**

A Terron uses four different ways to make purchases. What are they?

B Write the correct word next to its description. You will use some of the items two times.

cash   personal check   credit card   debit card

1. This is a written request to your bank asking them to pay money out of your account.

   _____

2. This allows you to borrow money to make purchases. _____

3. Coins and bills are this. _____

4. This allows a store to take money directly from your account to pay for

   purchases. _____

5. This allows you to buy now and pay later. _____

6. You can get cash out of the ATM with this. _____

30   Unit 2   Lesson 4

 LESSON **4** **GOAL** ➤ Identify and compare purchasing methods

C In groups, talk about the advantages and disadvantages of each purchasing method. Complete the chart below.

EXAMPLE: *Student A:* Cash is good because it is quick and easy.
Student B: Yes, but if you lose cash, you cannot replace it.

	Cash	Debit card	Personal check	Credit card
Advantages	quick and easy			
Disadvantages	can't replace			

D Talk to a partner about the purchasing method you prefer and why.

 CD 1 TR 6

E Listen to Terron and his wife, Leilani, talk about purchasing methods. Make a list of the things they *have to* do and *must* do.

Have to	Must

GOAL ➤ Identify and compare purchasing methods

F We use *must* and *have to* when something is necessary. *Must* is a little stronger than *have to*. Study the chart below with your teacher.

Must vs. *Have to*			
Subject	**Modal**	**Base verb**	
We	have to	save	money for vacation.
I	must	pay off	my credit card every month.

G Complete each statement with *must* or *have to* and a verb from the box.

> check   keep   put   make   pay

EXAMPLE: You ___must pay___ your bills if you want a good credit history.

1. You _____ _____ your cash in a safe place.

2. You _____ _____ track of the personal checks you write.

3. You _____ _____ the minimum amount on your credit card every month.

4. You _____ _____ sure you have enough money in the bank when you write a personal check.

5. You _____ _____ your balance before you get cash out of an ATM machine.

H Choose one purchasing method and write a paragraph on why you think it is better than all the rest. Use comparative and superlative adjectives.

_____

_____

_____

_____

_____

Think before you buy

GOAL ➤ Make a smart purchase

A Read about making smart purchases.

Making a Smart Purchase

You make a smart purchase when you think and plan before you buy something. First of all, you make a decision to buy something. This is the easy part. The second step is comparison shopping. You comparison shop by reading advertisements, going to different stores, and talking to friends and family. Third, you choose which product you are going to buy. Do you have enough money to buy this product? If you don't, the next step is to start saving. This may take a while depending on how much you need to save. Once you have enough money, you are ready to make your purchase. If you follow these steps to make a purchase, you will be a smart consumer. And smart consumers make smart purchases!

What is Leilani doing?
What is her problem?

B Put the steps in order from 1 to 5 according to the paragraph above.

_____ make the purchase

_____ read advertisements

___1___ decide to buy something

_____ choose the best deal

_____ save money

C Rewrite the steps in Exercise B after the words below.

First,   decide to buy something._____

Second,   _____.

Next,   _____.

Then,   _____.

Finally,   _____.

D *Sequencing transitions* are used to describe stages of a process. Study the examples in the box.

First,	First of all,	Second,	Second of all,	Third,
Fourth,	Next,	Then,	Lastly,	Finally,

E **Put the steps in the correct order.**

____ You decide to buy it.

____ You find out the price.

____ You see something in a store you want to buy.

____ You decide to charge it.

____ You think about if you have enough money to pay for it or not.

____ You pay for it.

____ You think about if you want to pay cash or put it on your credit card.

> *You*
>
> We use *you* to talk about people in general.

F Add sequencing transitions to the steps above to write a paragraph about making a purchase.

_____

_____

_____

_____

_____

_____

LESSON 5   **GOAL** ➤ **Make a smart purchase**

G Imagine you are going to buy a computer. In groups, come up with a list of steps to make a smart purchase.

> **Steps to Buying Our Computer**
>
> 1. _____
> 2. _____
> 3. _____
> 4. _____
> 5. _____
> 6. _____
> 7. _____
> 8. _____

H Write a paragraph about buying your computer. Use sequencing transitions.

_____

_____

_____

_____

_____

_____

_____

Review

A Where can you purchase the following goods or services? Write the places below. (Lesson 1)

Goods/Services	Place	Goods/Services	Place
1. shampoo	_____	6. a washing machine	_____
2. soccer ball	_____	7. fruit	_____
3. hammer	_____	8. a tune-up	_____
4. stamps	_____	9. clothes cleaned	_____
5. prescription refill	_____	10. shoes	_____

B Write the present tense form of *get* and the past participle of the verb in parentheses. (Lesson 1)

1. He ___gets___ his car ___washed___ at the local car wash. (wash)

2. She _____ her hair _____ at the hair salon. (cut)

3. He _____ his car _____ at the automotive shop. (clean)

4. They _____ their clothes _____ at the dry cleaners. (clean)

5. I _____ my checks _____ at the bank. (cash)

C Read the ads and answer the questions below. (Lesson 2)

1. Are these ads advertising the same thing? _____ If so, what? _____

2. What is the price of the car at Hill's? _____ At Albilene? _____

3. Which car is cheaper? _____

4. What is good about the offer from Hill's?_____

5. What is good about the offer from Albilene?_____

6. Which dealership would you buy from? _____

Why?_____

D Complete the following statements with a comparative or a superlative adjective. (Lesson 3)

1. My new watch was _____cheaper than_____ my old watch. (cheap)

2. This computer is _____ one in the store. (fast)

3. That mirror is _____ the one we have now. (tall)

4. This box is much _____ that one. What's in it? (heavy)

5. _____ paintings in the world are painted by that artist. (beautiful)

6. Do you think that the book is _____ the movie? (interesting)

7. Let's go to a different store. This is _____ one. (busy)

8. My neighbor's house is _____ our house. (big)

9. Do you think this car is _____ the one you have? (good)

E Imagine that you are going to buy a new car—your dream car. Write sentences comparing your old car to your new car. (Lesson 3)

EXAMPLE: My new car is faster than my old car. _____

_____

_____

_____

_____

F What is the best restaurant in your neighborhood? Write sentences comparing this restaurant to all the other restaurants in the neighborhood. (Lesson 3)

EXAMPLE: China Palace has the friendliest service in the neighborhood. _____

_____

_____

_____

_____

_____

Review

G Write a sentence about each of the following purchasing methods.
Use *must* or *have to*. (Lesson 4)

EXAMPLE: cashier's check: <u>You must be careful not to lose a cashier's check.</u>

1. cash: _____

2. personal check: _____

3. debit card: _____

4. credit card: _____

H Imagine that your friend is going to buy a new television. What steps would you tell him or her to take? Write them below. (Lesson 5)

1. _____

2. _____

3. _____

4. _____

5. _____

I Write a paragraph using the steps you wrote above. Use sequencing transitions. (Lesson 5)

_____

_____

_____

_____

_____

_____

_____

_____

_____

My Dictionary

Make flash cards to improve your vocabulary.

1. Choose four words from this unit.
2. Write each word on a 3-by-5 index card or on a piece of paper.
3. On the back of the card or paper, write a definition, or a sentence with the word missing, and draw a picture.
4. Study the words while you are traveling to school or work, or read them during breakfast. (Remember your time-management skills!) You can also ask a friend or family member to help you review.
5. Do this for each unit, and add other new words that you learn in or out of class. If you study a little each day, you will improve your vocabulary very quickly. By the end of this class, you will have a whole stack of flash cards!

Learner Log

In this unit, you learned many things about consumer smarts. How comfortable do you feel doing each of the skills listed below? Rate your comfort level on a scale of 1 to 4.

1 = Need more practice   **2** = OK   **3** = Good   **4** = Great!

Life Skill	Comfort Level				Page
I can identify places to purchase goods and services.	1	2	3	4	_____
I can interpret advertisements.	1	2	3	4	_____
I can compare products.	1	2	3	4	_____
I can identify and compare purchasing methods.	1	2	3	4	_____
I know how to make a smart purchase.	1	2	3	4	_____

If you circled 1 or 2, write down the page number where you can review this skill.

Reflection

1. What was the most useful skill you learned in this unit? _____

2. How will this help you in life? _____

Team Project

Create two advertisements and a purchase plan.

1. Form a team with four or five students. Choose positions for each member of your team.

POSITION	JOB DESCRIPTION	STUDENT NAME
Student 1: Leader	See that everyone speaks English. See that everyone participates.	
Student 2: Secretary	Write the advertisement. Take notes for the family.	
Student 3: Designer	Design advertisement layout.	
Students 4/5: Spokespeople	Plan presentations.	

Part 1—Advertising Team: Create Advertisements

1. Create two different advertisements for the same product or service. (Lesson 2)

2. Present your ads to the class and then post them in the classroom.

Part 2—Family: Create a Purchase Plan

1. Walk around the room and choose a product or service to buy from all the ads created by all the teams on the wall.

2. Compare two of the ads, writing four comparative statements about why one is better than the other. (Lessons 2–3)

3. Choose one product or service to buy and write a purchase plan—the steps needed to make a smart purchase. (Lessons 4–5)

4. Present your comparisons and purchase plan to the class.

Housing

GOALS

➤ Interpret classified ads
➤ Make decisions about housing

➤ Arrange and cancel utilities
➤ Make a budget
➤ Write a letter to a landlord

House hunting

GOAL ➤ Interpret classified ads

Vocabulary · Grammar · Life Skills · Academic · Pronunciation

A Think about the place where you live. How did you find it? What are some different ways to find housing?

B One way to find housing is through *classified ads* in the newspaper. Read the ads below. Which apartment do you like best?

FOR RENT

1.
Lge apartment,
2 floors, 3 bedrooms,
2 bath, gar, **pool,**
$1,500

2.
SUNNY
1 BR, 1 bath w/ huge l/r,
1 car gar, W/D, high ceilings,
security guard,
$895/mo.

3.
Charming 1BR condo,
1 bath, carport, large
balc, great condition,
carpeting, walk to ctr,
$800/mo.

4.
4 bdrm spacious condo,
pool, gar, laundry, nr school,
no pets, **$2,500/mo.**

5.
1st fl sunny studio,
yard, stove & frig, Cat OK,
first, last, & sec. dep,
$550 per month

6.
Clean 2 bedroom, 1 bath
apt in gated community
A/C, new appl, nr fwys
Gas, water, trash paid
avail 8/1, $1,195

C Work with a partner to list the abbreviations in the ads. What does each abbreviation stand for? Discuss their meanings with your teacher.

Abbreviation	Word	Meaning
lge	large	very big

GOAL ➤ Interpret classified ads

D Discuss the following questions about the ads on page 41 with your partner.

1. Which one-bedroom apartment has higher rent?
2. Which apartment has more rooms—#1 or #5?
3. Which apartment has more bathrooms—#1 or #6?

E Here are more ways to make comparisons. Study the charts below.

Comparatives Using Nouns	
Our new apartment has *more bedrooms* than our old one. Our old apartment had *fewer bedrooms* than our new one.	Use *more* or *fewer* to compare count nouns.
Rachel's apartment gets *more light* than Pablo's apartment. Pablo's apartment gets *less light* than Rachel's apartment.	Use *more* or *less* to compare noncount nouns.

Superlatives Using Nouns	
Rachel's apartment has *the most bedrooms*. Phuong's apartment has *the fewest bedrooms*.	Use *the most* or *the fewest* for count nouns.
Rachel's apartment has *the most light*. Phuong's apartment has *the least light*.	Use *the most* or *the least* for non-count nouns.

F Complete the sentences with the correct word: *more* or *most*.

1. Kim's house has _____ bedrooms than Jen's house.

2. The Worshams' apartment gets the _____ light.

3. That condo has _____ appliances than this one.

4. Her house has the _____ rooms.

G Complete the sentences with the correct word: *fewer, less, fewest,* or *least*.

1. John's house has _____ bathrooms than Brad's place.

2. The small condo has _____ light than the big one.

3. The small condo has the _____ space.

Vocabulary   **Grammar**
Life Skills
Academic   Pronunciation

FOR RENT

a.

Lge *apartment*,
1st floor, 2 bed, 1.5 bath,
gar, community spa,
sec dep $500, $975/month

c.

**BEAUTIFUL 3BR CONDO FOR RENT,
3 BATH, CARPORT FOR 2 CARS, LRG
PATIO, WOODS FLOORS, NR SHOPS,
SEC DEP $600, RENT $1,100/MO.**

Lge 5 BR, 2 bath **house**,
2 car gar, W/D hookups,
high ceilings, quiet nbhd.
sec dep $2,000, $2,000/mo. rent

Top fl bright studio,
balcony, new appl. Cat
OK, first, last, & sec. dep,
$550, $950 per month

b.

d.

H   **Work with a partner.** *Scan* the ads above and ask and answer the questions below. Try to answer in complete sentences.

1. Which place has more bathrooms, the house or the condo?

2. Which place has the most bedrooms?

3. Which place has the highest rent?

4. Which place has more bedrooms, the condo or the apartment?

5. Which place has the lowest security deposit?

> *Scan:* to quickly look for the answers in a text without reading everything

I   Write sentences comparing the places for rent.

EXAMPLES: <u>The studio has fewer rooms than the house.</u>

<u>The house has the most bedrooms.</u>

1. _____

2. _____

3. _____

4. _____

5. _____

6. _____

  J   **Active Task. Search** for classified ads for housing on the Internet. What abbreviations can you find? Tell the class. (Key words: housing ads *your city*)

Time to move

GOAL ➤ Make decisions about housing

(A) **Read about the Nguyen family.**

The Nguyen family lives in Cedarville, Texas. Vu Nguyen came from Vietnam twenty years ago and met his wife, Maryanne, in Texas. The Nguyens have four children—two sons and two daughters. They are currently living in a two-bedroom apartment, which is too small for all six of them. They would like to stay in Cedarville, but they need a bigger place. Vu recently got a raise at work, so the Nguyen family wants to move.

CD 1
TR 7

(B) **Listen to the Nguyen family talk about their housing preferences. Check the boxes next to the things they would like to have in their new apartment.**

☐ 2 bedrooms   ☐ tennis courts   ☐ yard
☐ 3 bedrooms   ☐ pool   ☐ air-conditioning
☐ 2 bathrooms   ☐ security guard   ☐ carpeting
☐ 3 bathrooms   ☐ big windows   ☐ balcony
☐ convenient location   ☐ carport   ☐ washer/dryer

(C) **Compare your answers with a partner.**

GOAL ➤ **Make decisions about housing**

D Study the chart with your classmates and teacher.

Yes/No Questions and Answers with *Do*				
Questions				**Short answers**
Do	**Subject**	**Base verb**	**Example question**	
do	I, you, we, they	have	Do they have a yard?	Yes, they do. / No, they don't.
does	he, she, it	want	Does she want air-conditioning?	Yes, she does. / No, she doesn't.

E Practice asking and answering *yes/no* questions with a partner, using the Nguyen family's preferences on page 44.

EXAMPLE: *Student A:* Do they want five bedrooms?
Student B: No, they don't.

Pronunciation

Yes/No **Questions:**
Rising Intonation

➤ Do they have a yard?

➤ Do you want five bedrooms?

➤ Does it have a balcony?

F Write five *yes/no* questions you could ask the Nguyens.

EXAMPLE: Do you want a bathtub?

1. _____

2. _____

3. _____

4. _____

5. _____

G With a partner, practice asking your questions with rising intonation.

GOAL ➤ Make decisions about housing

H Imagine you are going to buy or rent a new home. What kind of home do you want? Write the number of bedrooms and bathrooms you prefer. Then, check your preferences below. Add other preferences that are not on the list.

Yes No

_____ bedrooms

_____ bathrooms

❏ ❏ yard

❏ ❏ balcony

❏ ❏ pool

❏ ❏ washer/dryer

❏ ❏ air-conditioning

Yes No

❏ ❏ convenient location

❏ ❏ garage

❏ ❏ carport

❏ ❏ refrigerator

❏ ❏ _____

❏ ❏ _____

❏ ❏ _____

I Write five *yes/no* questions you can ask your partner about his or her housing preferences. Don't write the answers yet.

EXAMPLE: <u>Do you want a balcony?</u>

1. _____

Answer: _____

2. _____

Answer: _____

3. _____

Answer: _____

4. _____

Answer: _____

5. _____

Answer: _____

J Practice asking your questions with a partner. Use good rising intonation! Fill in the answers in Exercise I.

EXAMPLE: *Student A:* Do you want a balcony?
  Student B: Yes, I do.

Paying the bills

GOAL ➤ Arrange and cancel utilities

A Discuss these questions with your classmates.

1. What are utilities?

2. What utilities do you pay for?

3. Does your landlord pay for any utilities?

4. What information can you find on your utility bills?

✳ SOUTHERN TEXAS GAS ✳

P.O. Box D • Cedarville, TX 77014

Name Vu Nguyen
Service Address 3324 Maple Road, Cedarville, TX 77014
Account Number 891 007 1087 5   **Billing Period** 5/23/08-6/27/08

Readings: prev 4226   pres 4251

Summary of Charges

Customer Charge	33 days	x 0.16438=	5.42
Baseline	15 Therms	x0.65133=	9.77
Over Baseline	10 Therms	x0.82900=	8.29
Gas Charges			23.48
State Regulatory Fee	25 Therms	x0.00076=	.02
Taxes and Fees on Gas Charges			.02

Total Gas Charges Including Taxes and Fees	$23.50
Thank you for your payment Jun 06 2008	$27.65
Total Amount Due	**$23.50**

Current Amount Past Due if not paid by Jul 25, 2008
Next meter reading Jul 28, 2008

B Read the gas bill above and answer the questions below.

1. What is Vu's account number? _____

2. How much is their gas bill this month? _____

3. How much did they pay last month? _____

4. Which bill was more expensive—this month's or last month's? _____

5. Check the total amount of their bill. Is it correct? _____

6. When is the payment due? _____

  C Vu and his family are getting ready to move. Vu calls the electric company to speak to a customer service representative. Listen to the recording and write short answers for the following information.

CD 1
TR 8

1. Name of the company: _____

2. Name of the representative: _____

3. When Vu wants service turned off: _____

4. When Vu wants service turned on: _____

D Listen to the recording again and answer the questions.

CD 1
TR 8

1. The first voice is recorded and gives four choices. What are they?

    a. <u>get new service or cancel existing service</u>

    b. _____

    c. _____

    d. _____

2. What information does Vu give to the gas company?

    a. <u>his current address</u>

    b. _____

    c. _____

    d. _____

Pronunciation

Information Questions:
Rising and Falling Intonation

➤ What is your address?

➤ Where do you live?

➤ When will you be moving?

Information Questions	
Question words	**Example questions**
How	*How* may I help you?
What	*What* is your current address?
When	*When* would you like your service turned off?

 (E) **Read the conversation as you listen to the recording. Underline the information questions.**

CD 1
TR 9

Recording: Thank you for calling Southern Texas Gas. Your call is very important to us. Please wait for the next available customer service representative.

Representative: Hello, my name is Liam. How may I help you?
Vu: Um, yes. My family is moving next week and we need to have our gas turned off here and get the gas turned on in our new home.
Representative: What is your current address?
Vu: 3324 Maple Road.
Representative: What is your name sir?
Vu: Vu Nguyen.
Representative: When would you like the gas turned off?
Vu: Next Thursday, please.
Representative: And what is your new address?
Vu: 5829 Bay Road.
Representative: And when would you like the gas turned on in your new home?
Vu: This Monday, please.
Representative: OK. Your current service will be turned off sometime between 7 and 9 A.M. on Thursday the 12th, and your new service will be on before 8 on Monday morning, the 9th. Is there anything else I can do for you?
Vu: No, that's it.
Representative: Thank you for calling Southern Texas Gas. Have a nice day.
Vu: Thanks. You, too.

(F) Imagine you are moving. Write down your current address and a new address. What date will you leave your old home? What date will you move to your new home? With a partner, practice Vu's conversation using your own information. Remember to practice rising and falling intonation!

(G) With a partner, discuss ways to reduce the cost of your electric bill. What can you do to save energy?

LESSON 4

How much can we spend?

GOAL ➤ Make a budget

A What do you spend money on every month? Make a list.

	Monthly Expenses
rent	

B Share your list with a partner. Add anything to your list that you forgot.

C Listen to Maryanne and Vu talk about their finances. Fill in the missing information.

CD 1
TR 10

INCOME

Vu's Salary	$3,000
Maryanne's Salary	_____
Total Income	_____

EXPENSES

Rent	_____
Utilities	
Electricity	$60
Gas	_____
Telephone	$65 (average)
Cable TV	$55
Internet	$45
Groceries	_____
Auto	
Gas and maintenance	_____
Car loan	_____
Total Expenses	_____

Math Practice

TOTAL means addition (+).

$5.00	$47.00
+ $7.00	+ $36.00

$625.46	$4,734.00
+ $89.56	+ $5,902.00

$3,500.00	
+ $2,250.00	

D Answer the following questions about the Nguyens' budget with a partner.

1. What is their total income?

_____

2. What are their total expenses?

_____

3. How much extra cash do they have left after all the bills are paid? (*Hint:* Subtract total expenses from total income.)

_____

4. In your opinion, what are some things they forgot to budget for?

_____

5. What do you think they should do with their extra money? _____

_____

E Look at the bar graph for the Nguyen family's expenses. Complete the graph with their expenses from page 50. For this exercise do not include rent.

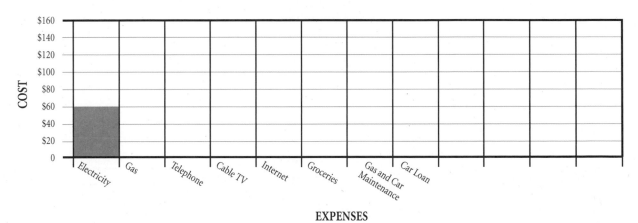

F Now include on the graph other items the Nguyen's should add to their budget and the budget amount for each.

GOAL ➤ Make a budget

G Work as a team to create a family budget. Use the following information:

➤ Your family has two adults and three children, ages two, five, and eight.

➤ You live in a four-bedroom house that you rent.

➤ Both adults have full-time jobs.

➤ You have two cars, one that you own (no payments) and the other that you lease.

Decide what your total household income is. Fill in the amounts that you would spend each month on expenses. Make a realistic budget based on your total income.

<u>**Monthly Budget**</u>

_____ Salary
_____ Salary
_____ Total Income

Expenses

Rent
Utilities
   Gas
   Telephone
   Cable TV
   Internet
Food
   Groceries
   Dining out
Entertainment
Auto
   Gas and maintenance
   Car loan
   Insurance
   Registration

<u>**Other**</u>

_____
_____
_____
_____

Total Expenses _____

H Prepare your own personal budget and make a bar graph.

Tenant rights

GOAL ➤ Write a letter to a landlord

A Look at the pictures below. Do you ever have these problems in your home? Are you a do-it-yourself person or do you call someone?

a. The air conditioner isn't working.

c. There are roaches and mice in the kitchen.

b. The electricity went out.

d. The faucet is leaking.

B Who can you call to fix each problem? Match the person with the problem.

1. __b__ electrician 3. _____ exterminator
2. _____ repairperson 4. _____ plumber

C Practice the conversation with a partner. Then, practice with the situations from Exercise A.

Tenant: Hello. This is <u>John</u> in Apartment 3B.
Landlord: Hi, <u>John</u>. What can I do for you?
Tenant: <u>The air-conditioning in our apartment isn't working.</u> (*State the problem.*)
Landlord: OK. I'll send <u>a repairperson over to fix it tomorrow.</u> (*State the solution.*)
Tenant: Thanks.

LESSON 5   **GOAL** ➤ **Write a letter to a landlord**

 D **Indira had a bad night in her apartment. Read about what happened.**

I had a terrible night. While I was making dinner, I saw a mouse. Then, the electricity went out while I was studying. It was dark, so I went to bed. But I couldn't sleep. The faucet was dripping all night. The neighbors were shouting and their dog was barking. Perhaps I should move!

E **Study the charts. Then, underline examples of the *past continuous* in the paragraph above.**

Past Continuous			
Subject	***be***	**Verb + *ing***	**Example sentence**
I, he, she, it	was	making	I was making breakfast.
you, we, they	were	studying	She was taking a shower.
Use the past continuous to talk about things that started in the past and continued for a period of time.			

Past Continuous Using *While*			
Subject	***be***	**Verb + *ing***	**Example sentence**
I, he, she, it	was	making	While I was making dinner, I saw a mouse.
you, we, they	were	studying	The electricity went out while we were studying.
To connect two events that happened in the past, use the past continuous with *while* for the longer event. Use the simple past for the shorter event.			
Note: You can reverse the two clauses, but you need a comma if the *while* clause comes first.			

F **Use *while* to combine the two sentences below. Read the sentences out loud.**

1. He was sleeping. The phone rang.

   <u>While he was sleeping, the phone rang.</u> OR <u>The phone rang while he was sleeping.</u>

2. Joshua was painting the cabinet. The shelf fell down.

   _____

3. I saw the crack in the wall. I was hanging a painting.

   _____

4. He was taking a shower. The water got cold.

   _____

5. The air-conditioning broke down. We were eating dinner.

   _____

GOAL ➤ Write a letter to a landlord

G Vu Nguyen had a problem when his family first moved into their new apartment. Read the letter that he wrote to his landlord.

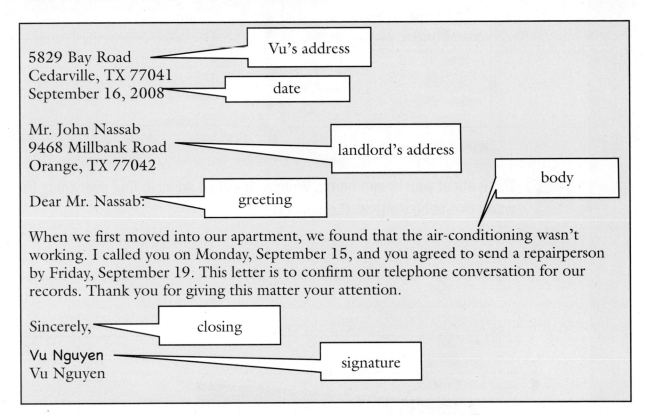

5829 Bay Road
Cedarville, TX 77041   *Vu's address*
September 16, 2008   *date*

Mr. John Nassab
9468 Millbank Road   *landlord's address*
Orange, TX 77042
                                                    body
Dear Mr. Nassab: *greeting*

When we first moved into our apartment, we found that the air-conditioning wasn't working. I called you on Monday, September 15, and you agreed to send a repairperson by Friday, September 19. This letter is to confirm our telephone conversation for our records. Thank you for giving this matter your attention.

Sincerely,   *closing*

Vu Nguyen
Vu Nguyen   *signature*

H What are the different parts of the letter? Discuss them with your teacher.

I Work with a partner to brainstorm problems you can have in an apartment. Write your ideas on a piece of paper and share them with the class.

J Write a letter to your landlord about a problem that you had in the past or a current problem you are having. Use Vu's letter as an example.

K Exchange letters with a partner. Check your partner's letter for grammar, spelling, and punctuation mistakes.

A Read the classified ad. Rewrite the ad with the full form of the abbreviations. (Lesson 1)

> **3BR** apt w/lg kitchen, 2 car gar, W/D, new appl, **nr beach**, $1,500/mo + $500 sec dep, Avail 8/30

_____

_____

_____

_____

_____

B Think about your dream home. Write a classified ad including everything that you would want. Use abbreviations. (Lesson 1)

_____

_____

_____

C Complete the sentences with the correct word: *more* or *most* (+); or *fewer, less, fewest,* or *least* (−). (Lesson 1)

1. (+) Kim's house has _____ more _____ entrances than Jen's house.

2. (+) The blue condo has _____ bathrooms than the yellow one.

3. (+) Octavio's apartment gets the _____ light.

4. (−) That condo has _____ balconies than this one.

5. (−) Their house has the _____ furniture.

6. (+) Andrew's place has _____ rooms than Brad's place.

7. (−) The small apartment has _____ patio space than the big one.

8. (+) The Jacksons' apartment has the _____ appliances.

9. (+) That house has _____ light than this one.

10. (−) His home has the _____ bathrooms.

D Write five *yes/no* questions to ask your partner about his or her dream home. Then ask your partner the questions and write the answers. (Lesson 2)

EXAMPLE: Q: <u>Do you want four bedrooms?</u>　　A: <u>No, I don't.</u>

1. Q: _____　A: _____

2. Q: _____　A: _____

3. Q: _____　A: _____

4. Q: _____　A: _____

5. Q: _____　A: _____

E Now look at the ad for your dream home that you wrote in Exercise B and the answers you just got from your partner. Write four sentences comparing the two dream homes. (Lesson 1)

EXAMPLE: <u>My partner's dream home has fewer bedrooms than my dream home.</u>

1. _____

_____

2. _____

_____

3. _____

_____

4. _____

_____

F Imagine you are moving to a new city. What utilities will you have to call and order? Write them below. With a partner, role-play a phone conversation with a customer service representative. (Lesson 3)

_____　　_____

_____　　_____

_____　　_____

Review

G Think about your monthly expenses and complete the budget below. (Lesson 4)

Income _____
_____ Salary _____
Total Income _____
Expenses
Rent _____
Utitilites _____
    Gas _____
    Telephone _____
    Cable TV _____
    Internet _____
Other _____
    Groceries _____
    Dining Out _____
    Entertainment _____
Auto
    Gas and maintenance _____
    Car loan _____
    Insurance _____
    Registration _____
Total Expenses _____

H Use the simple past or the past continuous to complete the sentences. (Lesson 5)

1. The light _____**went out**_____ (go out) while Maryanne

   _____**was taking**_____ (take) a shower.

2. A spider _____ (drop) onto my arm while I

   _____ (eat) dinner.

3. While Marie _____ (study), the landlord

   _____ (call).

4. While Terry _____ (clean) the window, he

   _____ (hurt) his back.

5. Someone _____ (break) into their house

   while they _____ (visit) friends.

I Think of some problems you have had with the place that you are living in. On a piece of paper, use one of your ideas to write a letter to your landlord. (Lesson 5)

My Dictionary

Study with a partner.

1. Go back through the unit. Highlight ten new words that you want to study.
2. Write each word on a 3-by-5 index card or on a small piece of paper.
3. Work in pairs. Your partner chooses one card and asks questions to help you guess the word on the card.
4. Switch roles and continue until all the words have been reviewed.

> EXAMPLE: *Student A:* Who collects the rent? OR Who owns your apartment?
> *Student B:* Tenant?
> *Student A:* No, try again.
> *Student B:* Landlord?
> *Student A:* That's right.

Learner Log

In this unit, you learned many things about housing. How comfortable do you feel doing each of the skills listed below? Rate your comfort level on a scale of 1 to 4.

1 = Need more practice   **2** = OK   **3** = Good   **4** = Great!

Life Skill	Comfort Level				Page
I can interpret classified ads.	1	2	3	4	_____
I can make decisions about housing.	1	2	3	4	_____
I can arrange and cancel utilities.	1	2	3	4	_____
I can interpret utility bills.	1	2	3	4	_____
I can budget household expenses.	1	2	3	4	_____
I can write a letter to a landlord.	1	2	3	4	_____

If you circled 1 or 2, write down the page number where you can review this skill.

Reflection

1. What was the most useful skill you learned in this unit? _____

_____

2. How will this help you in life? _____

Team Project

Create a housing plan.

With a team, you will create a housing plan, including a budget and classified ad of where you will live.

1. Form a team with four or five students. You are now a family. Choose positions for each member of your team.

POSITION	JOB DESCRIPTION	STUDENT NAME
Student 1: Leader	See that everyone speaks English. See that everyone participates.	
Student 2: Secretary	Write the classified ad.	
Student 3: Financial Planner	Create the budget.	
Students 4/5: Family Representatives	Plan a presentation of your housing plan.	

2. Think about your family's needs. Create your family budget. (Lesson 4)

3. Think of a place that will be perfect for your family. Create your classified ad. (Lessons 1–2)

4. Make a list of all the utilities you will need to arrange for. (Lesson 3)

5. Create a poster with artwork. Include your budget, classified ad, and list of utilities.

6. Present your poster to the class.

Our Community

GOALS

➤ Ask for information
➤ Interpret charts and compare information

➤ Interpret a road map
➤ Identify daily activities
➤ Write about a place

LESSON **1**

Places in your community

GOAL ➤ Ask for information

Vocabulary · Grammar · Life Skills · Academic · Pronunciation

CD 1
TR 11

A Gloria and her family are new to the community. Read her list of things to do. Where does Gloria need to go for each one? Listen and write the names of the places below.

Things to Do

1. Find a place for my children to play sports _____

2. Register for an ESL class _____

3. Open a checking account _____

4. Register my car and get a new license _____

5. Find a place for my children to use computers _____

6. Pick up some bus schedules _____

B Practice the conversation with a partner, using the information from Exercise A.

EXAMPLE: *Student A:* Where can I <u>get a new driver's license</u>?
Student B: At the <u>DMV</u>.

DMV = Department of
Motor Vehicles

 Study the chart.

Information Questions		
Location	Where	is the bank?
	How far	is the school from here?
	What	is the address?
Time	When	does the library open?
	What time	does the restaurant close?
	How often	do the buses run?
Cost	How much	does it cost?

D Match the questions you could ask when calling a local business with the correct answers.

Questions

_g_ 1. How often do the buses run?

___ 2. Where is your restaurant?

___ 3. How much does it cost?

___ 4. What is your address?

___ 5. What time do you close?

___ 6. How far is the store from here?

___ 7. When do you open?

___ 8. What time do you close on Sunday?

Answers

a. We open at 10 A.M.

b. Our store is about five miles away.

c. We close at 10 P.M.

d. We're open from 10 to 6 on Sunday.

e. We are located at 71 South Pine Ave.

f. We're on the corner of 7th and Pine.

g. They run every 20 minutes.

h. It costs $50 to service your computer.

 Practice asking and answering the questions above with a partner. Remember to use rising and falling intonation.

Pronunciation

Information Questions:
Rising and Falling Intonation

➤ What time does the bank open?

➤ How much does it cost?

➤ What is the address?

GOAL ➤ **Ask for information**

F Help Gloria think of questions she needs to ask when she calls local businesses. Write questions to match the answers below.

1. What time does the bank open?   The bank opens at 9:00 A.M.

2. _____   A driver's license costs $25.

3. _____   The library is about a mile from here.

4. _____   The trains run every ten minutes.

5. _____   You can return books anytime.

6. _____   The DMV is at 112 Main Street.

7. _____   The children's book section is upstairs.

G Complete the conversations below with a logical question or answer. When you are finished, practice the conversations with a partner.

Conversation 1

A: Good morning. This is Food Mart.

B: _____

A: We're open now.

B: Great! Thank you.

Conversation 2

A: Thank you for calling The Book Stop. How can I help you?

B: _____

A: 4635 Broadway.

B: And when do you close?

A: _____

B: Thanks!

H On a piece of paper, make your own to-do list like the one Gloria made on page 61. Next to each item, write the place where you can go in your community to get the task done. Also, write some questions to ask. Look at the example below.

To Do	Place	Question
get information about ESL classes	an adult-education center	When do classes start? Where is the school?

LESSON 2

The bank, the library, and the DMV

GOAL ➤ Interpret charts and compare information

A Write the places.

1. open an account _____

2. register your car _____

3. check out books _____

4. get a driver's license _____

5. make a deposit _____

6. use a computer _____

B What is the name of your bank? What kind of bank account do you have? Discuss the following words with your classmates and teacher.

service fee   direct deposit   unlimited check writing   ATM

transactions   minimum balance   teller

C Riverview Bank offers three kinds of checking accounts. Read the brochure below.

RIVERVIEW BANK	Premiere	Express	Standard
Service Fee with direct deposit	$22	$0	$8
without direct deposit	$20	$7	$10
Check Writing	unlimited	20 per month	unlimited
ATM Transactions	unlimited	unlimited	unlimited
Teller Transactions	unlimited	$2 for each transaction	$4 fee per month
Other Information	no service fee if account balance is over $10,000	no minimum balance	no minimum balance

D With a partner, practice asking questions about the bank brochure above.

1. What is the service fee without direct deposit for the _____ account?

2. How many checks can you write per month with the _____ account?

3. How many ATM transactions can you have per month with the _____ account?

GOAL ➤ Interpret charts and compare information

E Read the following brochure about library services. You may not understand every word or phrase, but see if you can get the general idea.

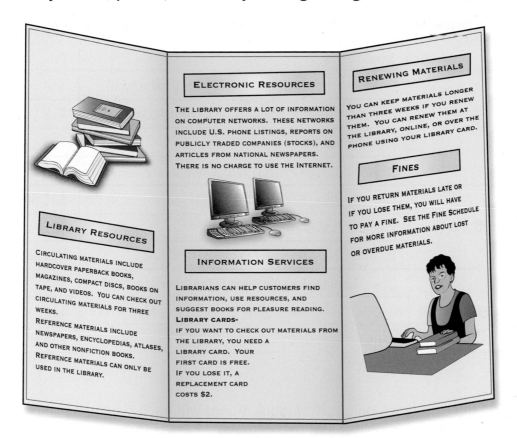

ELECTRONIC RESOURCES

THE LIBRARY OFFERS A LOT OF INFORMATION ON COMPUTER NETWORKS. THESE NETWORKS INCLUDE U.S. PHONE LISTINGS, REPORTS ON PUBLICLY TRADED COMPANIES (STOCKS), AND ARTICLES FROM NATIONAL NEWSPAPERS. THERE IS NO CHARGE TO USE THE INTERNET.

RENEWING MATERIALS

YOU CAN KEEP MATERIALS LONGER THAN THREE WEEKS IF YOU RENEW THEM. YOU CAN RENEW THEM AT THE LIBRARY, ONLINE, OR OVER THE PHONE USING YOUR LIBRARY CARD.

FINES

IF YOU RETURN MATERIALS LATE OR IF YOU LOSE THEM, YOU WILL HAVE TO PAY A FINE. SEE THE FINE SCHEDULE FOR MORE INFORMATION ABOUT LOST OR OVERDUE MATERIALS.

LIBRARY RESOURCES

CIRCULATING MATERIALS INCLUDE HARDCOVER PAPERBACK BOOKS, MAGAZINES, COMPACT DISCS, BOOKS ON TAPE, AND VIDEOS. YOU CAN CHECK OUT CIRCULATING MATERIALS FOR THREE WEEKS.
REFERENCE MATERIALS INCLUDE NEWSPAPERS, ENCYCLOPEDIAS, ATLASES, AND OTHER NONFICTION BOOKS. REFERENCE MATERIALS CAN ONLY BE USED IN THE LIBRARY.

INFORMATION SERVICES

LIBRARIANS CAN HELP CUSTOMERS FIND INFORMATION, USE RESOURCES, AND SUGGEST BOOKS FOR PLEASURE READING.
LIBRARY CARDS-
IF YOU WANT TO CHECK OUT MATERIALS FROM THE LIBRARY, YOU NEED A LIBRARY CARD. YOUR FIRST CARD IS FREE. IF YOU LOSE IT, A REPLACEMENT CARD COSTS $2.

F Decide if these statements are true or false based on the information in the library brochure. Fill in the circle. Then, change each false statement to make it true.

	True	False
cannot 1. You ~~can~~ check out reference materials.	○	●
2. Librarians can suggest books to read.	○	○
3. You can check out circulating materials.	○	○
4. The library has a database of phone listings from all over the world.	○	○
5. Your first library card costs $2.	○	○
6. You can renew materials over the phone using a driver's license.	○	○
7. You can check out library materials for three weeks.	○	○
8. If a book is late, it is overdue and you must pay a fine.	○	○
9. There is a fee to use the Internet.	○	○

GOAL ➤ Interpret charts and compare information

(G) Have you been to the DMV in your city? If so, why did you go there? Did you have to pay for services? Look at the chart of DMV fees below.

DMV Fees			
	Type	Fee	Valid
NEW	Driver License, Regular Class C (non-commercial)	$54.50	8 years
	Instruction Permit, Regular Class C (non-commercial)	$18	2 years
	Identification Card	$29	8 years
	Disabled Person Parking Permit, Temporary	No Fee	8 years
RENEWAL	Driver License, Regular Class C (non-commercial)	$34.50	NA
	Identification Card	$25	NA
	Disabled Person Parking Permit, Temporary	No Fee	
REPLACEMENT	Driver License, Regular Class C (non-commercial)	$21	NA
	Instruction Permit, Regular Class C (non-commercial)	$18	NA
	Identification Card	$24	NA

(H) Read the sentences below. How much money will each person have to pay at the DMV?

1. Enrico needs to get a new ID card. $_____

2. Liza lost her instruction permit and she needs to get a new one. $_____

3. Peter's driver's license expired and he needs to get a new one. $_____

4. Kim and Claudia just learned how to drive and they both need to get new driver's licenses. $_____

5. Gertrude needs a disabled person parking permit. $_____

(I) Imagine that you have to create a brochure for new students at your school. Work with a group to list all the important information to include.

Finding Places

GOAL ➤ Interpret a road map

 A Discuss these questions with your classmates.

1. How far do you live from your school in miles?

2. What are some major freeways or interstates in your area? What directions do they run?

3. Where is your school located? What are the nearest towns or cities? Where are they in relation to your school?

B Gloria and her family lived in Lindon. They decided to move to Victoria because Victoria has better schools and safer neighborhoods. This is a map of the area where they live. Look at the map. Then, answer the questions on page 68.

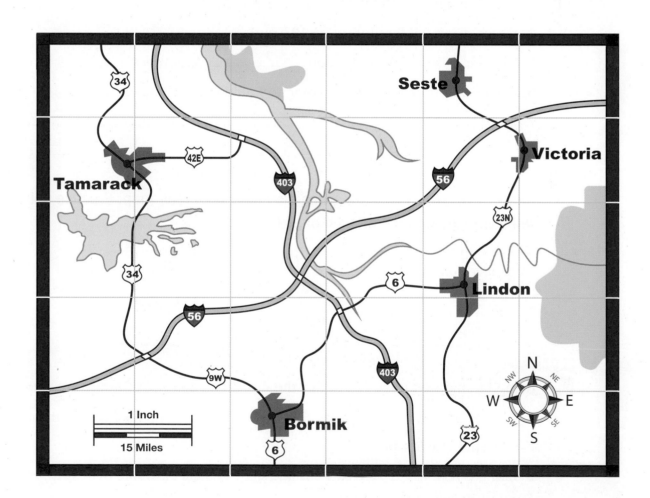

C Work in pairs. Answer the questions below using the map on page 67. Then, ask two more questions of your own.

EXAMPLE: *Student A:* Where is Lindon in relation to Victoria?
    Student B: It is southwest of Victoria.

1. How far is Lindon from Victoria? _____ miles

2. What freeway is Victoria closest to? _____ What direction does this

    freeway run? _____

3. Gloria also considered moving her family to Tamarack. Where is this city

    located in relation to Lindon? _____

4. Which direction does Interstate 403 run? _____

5. How far is Bormik from Lindon? _____ miles

6. Where is Bormik located in relation to Lindon? _____

7. _____

8. _____

D Study these expressions for giving directions on a road map. Practice pointing with your finger on the map on page 67.

Go north on 403.	**Exit at** Seste.
Take 56 West.	**Get off at** Exit 48 in Bormik.
Get on 34 North.	

E Using the map on page 67, follow the directions below. What city are you near?

1. Take 403 North to 6 East. At Lindon, get on 23 North. Take 23 North and go

    past Highway 56. What city are you in? _____

2. Take 403 South to 42 East. At Tamarack, take 34 South. Take 56 East to 403 South.

    Get on Highway 6 going south. What city are you in? _____

3. Take 6 North until it turns into 9 West. Then get on 56 East. Cross 403 and

    go about 40 miles. What city is to the south? _____

F Look at the city map. How is it different from the map on page 67?

G Study these expressions for giving directions in a city.

Go straight for three blocks.	It's **next to** the bank.
Turn left. / **Make a** left.	It's **across from** the park.
Take Second Avenue to Oak Street.	It's **on the corner of** First and Main.

H Read the directions below and follow them on the map with your finger.

Start at the subway station on Fifth Avenue. Take a right out of the station. Turn left on Main Street. Go straight for three blocks. Take a left on Second Avenue. It's at the corner of Oak and Second Avenue. What's the name of the building? _____

I Give your partner directions to different places on the two maps. Start your conversations using the questions below.

How can I get to	Tarmack	from	Seste?
	Bormik		Victoria?
	the subway station		the post office?
	the art museum		the Japanese restaurant?

Getting things done!

GOAL ➤ **Identify daily activities**

A Look at the picture and read about Gloria's busy day.

Yesterday was a busy day! After I woke up, I got the kids ready for school. Before my husband left for work, I ironed his shirt. When everyone left the house, I made my list of errands and off I went. First, I returned some books to the library. I stopped by the bank to make a deposit after I returned the books. Then, I went to the post office to mail a package to my family back in Brazil. The next errand on my list was grocery shopping. But before I went grocery shopping, I remembered to go to the cleaners and pick up some skirts. Finally, when I finished shopping, I went home. It was a long morning!

B Number in the correct order.

_____ picked up dry cleaning

_____ got the kids ready for school

_____ ironed husband's shirt

_____ left the house

_____ made a deposit at the bank

___1___ woke up

_____ made a list of errands

_____ mailed a package at the post office

_____ returned books to the library

_____ went grocery shopping

C *Before, after,* and *when* are used to connect two ideas and show their relationship in time. These words begin adverbial time clauses.

Adverbial Clauses with *Before, After,* and *When*	
Example	**Rule**
After I returned the books, I stopped by the bank to make a deposit.	The action closest to *after* happened first. (First, she returned the books. Second, she went to the bank.)
Before I went grocery shopping, I stopped by the cleaners to pick up some skirts.	The action closest to *before* happened second. (First, she went to the cleaners. Second, she went grocery shopping.)
When everyone left the house, I made my list of errands and off I went.	The action closest to *when* is completed and then next act begins. (First, everyone left. Second, she made her list.)
I went home **when** I finished shopping. **When** I finished shopping, I went home.	You can reverse the two clauses and the meaning stays the same. You need a comma if the adverbial clause goes first.

D In each of these sentences, underline the action that happened first.

EXAMPLE: After <u>I woke up</u>, I made breakfast.

1. I stopped by the bank to make a deposit before I returned the books.

2. Before Wendy went shopping, she went to the gym.

3. When my kids came home, I made dinner.

E Rewrite each sentence above, switching the order of the two actions.

EXAMPLE: **After** I woke up, I made breakfast.

<u>I made breakfast after I woke up.</u>

1. _____

2. _____

3. _____

F Talk with your partner. In the sentences you wrote above, which action happened first?

Pronunciation

Phrasing
➤ **Phrasing** is taking a pause or breath in the middle of a sentence.
➤ **We usually pause between two thoughts or when there is a comma.**
             pause
➤ When my kids came home, I made dinner.
            pause
➤ She went to the store before she picked up the dry cleaning.

G Write sentences with adverbial clauses. Use the words in parentheses. Then, rewrite the sentences, reversing the clauses.

EXAMPLE: Ali finished work. He went out with his friends. (when)

a. When Ali finished work, he went out with his friends.

b. Ali went out with his friends when he finished work.

1. Yasu saved enough money. He bought a new bicycle. (after)

    a. _____

    b. _____

2. The alarm went off. Maya jumped out of bed. (when)

    a. _____

    b. _____

H List five things you did yesterday in the order in which you did them. Then, write three sentences using *before, after,* or *when* to talk about your day.

1. _____   Yesterday

   _____   1. _____

2. _____   2. _____

   _____   3. _____

3. _____   4. _____

   _____   5. _____

My town

GOAL ➤ Write about a place

A Gloria is writing a paragraph about Victoria. Read her brainstorming notes below.

Reasons I love Victoria

safe neighborhoods (kids play in park)   affordable housing (can buy new house)

good schools (nationally recognized)   ~~good shopping~~

~~mild weather (never gets too cold or hot)~~   good job opportunities (computer industry)

> **_Brainstorm:_** to write a list of ideas you might use in your paragraph

B Gloria decided to focus on a few of the ideas for her paragraph. She wrote the six sentences below, but they are not in the correct order. Choose the best topic sentence and write *1* in front of it. Choose the best conclusion sentence and write *6* in front of it. Then, choose the order of the support sentences and number them 2–5. (Look at page 8 to review the different parts of a paragraph.)

____ Thanks to the great job market in Victoria, my husband got an excellent position in a computer company.

____ Our family can buy a nice house because the housing prices are very affordable here.

____ I love Victoria so much that I can't imagine moving.

____ The neighborhoods are very safe and so I can let my children play in the park with other children.

____ The excellent schools in this area are nationally recognized.

____ There are many reasons I love my new hometown Victoria.

GOAL ➤ **Write about a place**

C Now compose a paragraph, using Gloria's sentences in Exercise B. Use transitions from the box below to connect your support sentences. Write a title for Gloria's paragraph on the top line.

First of all,	Second,	Also,
First,	Third,	Finally,
Second of all,	Furthermore,	

_____

_____

_____

_____

_____

_____

_____

_____

_____

_____

_____

D Now think about your town. Follow each step below.

1. Brainstorm at least six reasons why you like your town.

EXAMPLE: _____ friendly people _____

Reasons I love _____

friendly people

GOAL ➤ **Write about a place**

2. Choose four of your reasons about why you like your town to include in your paragraph.

3. Write a topic sentence for your paragraph.

_____

_____

_____

4. Write four support sentences based on the four reasons you chose.

a. _____

_____

_____

b. _____

_____

_____

c. _____

_____

_____

d. _____

_____

_____

5. Write a conclusion sentence.

_____

_____

_____

 E On a piece of paper, write a paragraph about your town or city, using your work in Exercise D. Use transitions to connect your ideas.

Review

A Where can you do the following things in your community? (Lesson 1)

1. have lunch _____

2. get medicine _____

3. mail a letter _____

4. get cash _____

B What are some questions you might ask at the places you wrote in Exercise A? Write a question for each place. (Lesson 1)

1. _____

2. _____

3. _____

4. _____

C Look back at the Riverview Bank brochure on page 64. Read about the following people and decide which checking account would be best for each. Write the account name on the line. (Lesson 2)

1. Vu likes to do all of his banking at an ATM machine. He rarely goes inside the bank. His company deposits his paycheck automatically. He writes about 15 checks a month. Which account is best for Vu?

    _____

2. Mario likes to go inside the bank and do his transactions with a teller. He doesn't trust ATM machines. He also writes a lot of checks, so he's looking for an account that allows him unlimited check writing. He likes to keep at least $2,500 in his account. Which account is best for Mario?

    _____

3. Gloria and her husband want to buy a new house. They currently have $15,600 in the bank. They pay a lot of bills each month by check, so they want unlimited check writing. Gloria likes to do her banking with a teller. However, her husband works during banking hours and needs to use an ATM machine. Which account is best for Gloria and her husband?

    _____

D Draw a map showing the way from your school to a nearby restaurant. Then, write the directions. Read the directions to your partner and see if your partner can draw a map. (Lesson 3)

Draw your map here:

Write your directions here:

_____

_____

_____

_____

_____

_____

_____

_____

_____

_____

_____

_____

E Write sentences with adverbial clauses. Use *before, after,* or *when.* (Lesson 4)

EXAMPLE: I woke up. I made breakfast.

After I woke up, I made breakfast.

1. The children finished breakfast. I got them ready for school.

_____

2. I got some money out of the ATM. I bought some groceries.

_____

3. Mala finished work. She went to the movies.

_____

4. Luigi graduated from college. He got a job in a computer company.

_____

F Ask your partner why he or she likes the city he or she lives in. Write four reasons below. (Lesson 5)

Reasons I love _____

G Write a short paragraph about your partner's city. Don't forget to use transitions. (Lesson 5)

H Share the paragraph with your partner. Have your partner find the topic sentence, support sentences, and conclusion sentence. (Lesson 5)

My Dictionary

Write down ten new words you learned in this unit. Put them in alphabetical order. Then, look up the words in your dictionary to see if you were correct. Write sentences to help you remember the most difficult words.

1.   6.

2.   7.

3.   8.

4.   9.

5.   10.

Sentences: _____

_____

_____

Learner Log

In this unit, you learned many things about communities. How comfortable do you feel doing each of the skills listed below? Rate your comfort level on a scale of 1 to 4.

1 = Need more practice   **2** = OK   **3** = Good   **4** = Great!

Life Skill	Comfort Level	Page
I can ask for information.	1 2 3 4	_____
I can interpret charts.	1 2 3 4	_____
I can compare information.	1 2 3 4	_____
I can interpret road and street maps.	1 2 3 4	_____
I can give and receive directions.	1 2 3 4	_____
I can identify daily activities.	1 2 3 4	_____
I can write about my town.	1 2 3 4	_____

If you circled 1 or 2, write down the page number where you can review this skill.

Reflection

1. What was the most useful skill you learned in this unit?

_____

2. How will this help you in life?

_____

Team Project

Create a community brochure.

Imagine that a new family has moved into your neighborhood and you want to tell them all about your community. With your team, you will create a brochure about your community.

1. Form a team with four or five students. Choose a position for each member of your team.

POSITION	JOB DESCRIPTION	STUDENT NAME
Student 1: Leader	See that everyone speaks English. See that everyone participates.	
Student 2: Writer	Write information for brochure.	
Student 3: Designer	Design brochure layout and add artwork.	
Students 4/5: City Representatives	Help writer and designer with their work.	

2. Make a list of everything you want to include in your brochure, for example, information about the library, banks, and other local services. (Lessons 1–2)

3. Create the text for your community brochure. (Lessons 1–2, 5)

4. Create a map of your community. (Lesson 3)

5. Create artwork for your community brochure.

6. Present your brochure to the class.

Health

GOALS

➤ **Identify parts of the body**
➤ **Communicate symptoms to a doctor**
➤ **Identify health habits**

➤ **Interpret nutrition information**
➤ **Interpret fitness information**

LESSON 1

The human body

GOAL ➤ Identify parts of the body

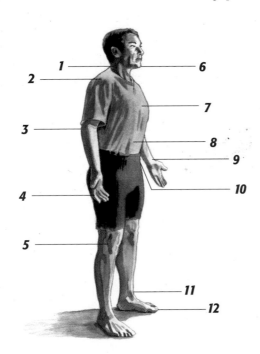

wrist	~~neck~~	shoulder
ankle	chest	toe
hip	stomach	elbow
knee	finger	chin

A Label the parts of the human body using the words from the box.

1. ___neck___   4. _____   7. _____   10. _____

2. _____   5. _____   8. _____   11. _____

3. _____   6. _____   9. _____   12. _____

B What other parts of the body can you name? Work with a partner. Label other parts of the body by drawing a line from the body part and writing its name.

C Match the doctor with the specialization. Ask your teacher for help with answers and pronunciation. Write your answers in the chart below. Add one more to the list.

Doctors	Specialization
1. __c__ podiatrist	a. allergies and asthma
2. _____ dermatologist	b. children
3. _____ gynecologist/obstetrician	c. feet
4. _____ cardiologist	d. teeth
5. _____ ophthalmologist	e. mental illness
6. _____ pediatrician	f. heart
7. _____ dentist	g. eyes
8. _____ allergist	h. women and childbirth
9. _____ psychiatrist	i. skin
10. _____ _____	j. _____

D Talk with a partner. Use the statements below to make recommendations about which type of doctor to see.

EXAMPLE: *Student A:* My mother's feet hurt.
Student B: She should see a podiatrist.

1. My father is worried about his heart. _____

2. My six-year-old son has a fever. _____

3. My nose is running and my eyes are itchy. _____

4. My eyes hurt when I read. _____

5. I feel depressed. _____

6. I have a rash on my neck. _____

7. I think I have a cavity. _____

8. My sister thinks she is pregnant. _____

9. _____ _____

GOAL ➤ **Identify parts of the body**

Vocabulary | Grammar
Life Skills
Academic | Pronunciation

E Look at the illustration of the internal parts of the human body. Review the pronunciation of new words with your teacher.

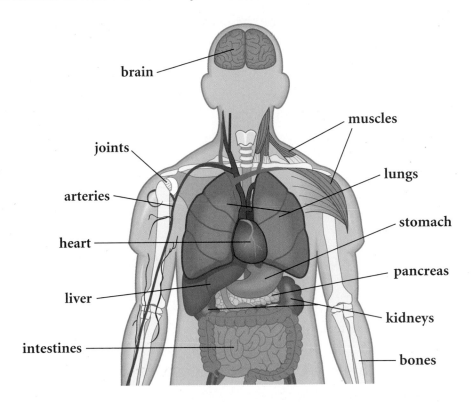

brain
muscles
joints
arteries
lungs
heart
stomach
liver
pancreas
intestines
kidneys
bones

F Can you talk to your doctor about your medical history? Match the condition or disease with the correct part of the body. Then, add one idea of your own.

Condition or disease	Part of body
1. _b_ high blood pressure	a. brain
2. ___ asthma	b. heart and arteries
3. ___ ulcers	c. joints
4. ___ stroke	d. stomach
5. ___ arthritis	e. lungs
6. _____	f. _____

Illnesses and symptoms

GOAL ➤ Communicate symptoms to a doctor

A Read the conversation and answer the questions.

Doctor: What seems to be the problem?
Ali: I have a terrible backache.
Doctor: I see. How long have you had this backache?
Ali: I've had it for about a week.
Doctor: Since last Monday?
Ali: Yes, that's right.

1. What is the matter with Ali? _____

2. When did his problem start? _____

B Make similar conversations using the information below.

EXAMPLES:
Student A: What's the matter?
Student B: I <u>feel dizzy</u>.
Student A: How long <u>have you felt dizzy</u>?
Student B: <u>For two days</u>.

Student A: What's the matter?
Student B: <u>My back hurts</u>.
Student A: How long <u>has your back hurt</u>?
Student B: <u>Since yesterday</u>.

Base Verb	Past Participle
be	been
have	had
feel	felt
hurt	hurt

1. I have a headache. (five hours)

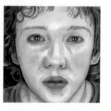

2. My eyes are red. (last night)

3. My shoulder hurts. (two weeks)

4. I feel tired. (Monday)

5. My throat is sore. (three days)

GOAL ➤ Communicate symptoms to a doctor

C Study the charts with your teacher.

Present Perfect					
Subject	*have*	Past participle		Time	Example sentence
I, you we, they	have	been	sick	since Tuesday	I *have been* sick since Tuesday.
she, he, it	has	had	a backache	for two weeks	She *has had* a backache for two weeks.
Use the present perfect for events starting in the past and continuing up to the present.					

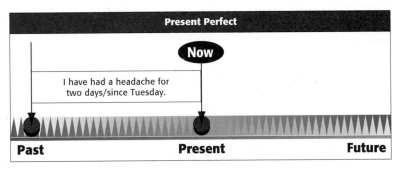

Present Perfect

Now

I have had a headache for two days/since Tuesday.

Past   Present   Future

Length of Time	Point in Time
for ...	*since ...*
five minutes	last night
three days	Thursday
one week	November
two years	1998
a long time	I was a child

D Complete the sentences with the present perfect of the verb in parentheses and *for* or *since*.

1. She _____ (be) tired _____ last week.

2. John's leg _____ (be) sore _____ three days.

3. Karen _____ (have) a sore throat _____ last night.

4. I _____ (feel) sick _____ Monday.

5. The girl's arm _____ (hurt) _____ two days.

6. The twins _____ (be) sick _____ a week.

GOAL ➤ **Communicate symptoms to a doctor**

E Make sentences using the present perfect and *for* or *since*.

EXAMPLE: Ali has a backache / Monday

<u>Ali has had a backache since Monday.</u>

1. I have a cold / three days

_____

2. my leg hurts / last night

_____

3. Julie feels dizzy / a week

_____

4. Peter is sick / two weeks

_____

5. they are ill / a long time

_____

6. our allergies are bad / we were five years old

_____

F Work in pairs. Write symptoms for each illness below.

Illness	Symptoms
a cold	
the flu	
a cough	
allergies	
depression	

G With your partner, role-play a conversation between a doctor and a patient. Choose an illness from the chart above and ask questions about the symptoms. Remember to use *how long* and the present perfect.

Health habits

GOAL ➤ **Identify health habits**

A Look at the picture. What are the people doing? What is healthy and what is unhealthy?

> healthy = good for your mind and body
>
> unhealthy = bad for your mind and body

B Health habits are actions that affect your health, such as drinking water (a good habit) or smoking (a bad habit). Read and match each health habit to an effect below. There may be more than one answer. Compare answers with a partner.

Health habit (Cause)

1. __j__ be very stressed
2. ___ drink too much alcohol
3. ___ stay in the sun too long
4. ___ eat junk food every day
5. ___ exercise at least three times a week
6. ___ don't get enough calcium
7. ___ don't sleep eight hours every night
8. ___ smoke too much
9. ___ stay away from smoking
10. ___ wear sunscreen

Effect

a. have healthy lungs

b. not be well rested

c. destroy your liver

d. not have strong bones

e. get lung cancer

f. protect your skin

g. get skin cancer

h. be fit and healthy

i. gain weight

j. have high blood pressure

GOAL ➤ Identify health habits

C Study the chart with your teacher.

Future Conditional Statements	
Cause: *If* + present tense	**Effect: future tense**
If you *are* very stressed,	you *will have* high blood pressure.
If you *don't eat* enough calcium,	you *won't have* strong bones.
We can connect a cause and an effect by using a *future conditional* statement. The *if*-clause (or the *cause*) is in the present tense and the *effect* is in the future tense.	
Effect: future tense	**Cause: *if* + present tense**
You *will have* high blood pressure	*if* you *are* very stressed.
You can reverse the clauses, but use a comma only when the *if*-clause comes first.	

D Complete the sentences with the correct forms of the verbs in parentheses.

1. If you _____wash_____ (wash) your hands a few times a day, you _____won't get_____ (not get) so many colds.

2. If Ann _____ (get) her teeth cleaned regularly, she _____ (not have) so many cavities.

3. My dad _____ (not lose) weight if he _____ (keep) eating foods that are high in fat.

4. My skin _____ (burn) if I _____ (not use) sunscreen.

5. If people _____ (not stretch) before they exercise, they _____ (have) sore muscles.

6. If you _____ (drink) too much beer, you _____ (get) a big stomach.

7. If Susan _____ (not eat) before she runs her race, she _____ (pass out).

8. Araceli _____ (lose) the weight she gained when she was pregnant if she

   _____ (walk) with her baby every day.

9. Bang Vu _____ (not be able to) talk tomorrow if he _____ (not rest) his voice.

E With a partner, practice making conditional statements with the information from Exercise B on page 87. Use different subjects (*I, you, we, they, he, she, it*).

EXAMPLE: If we smoke cigarettes, we will get lung cancer.

1. _____

2. _____

3. _____

4. _____

5. _____

6. _____

F Think about your good and bad health habits. Make two lists.

My *Good* Health Habits	My Bad Health Habits

G Write four future conditional statements about good health habits you would like to have. Then, read them to your partner.

EXAMPLE: If I get more sleep, I will concentrate better on my work.

1. _____

2. _____

3. _____

4. _____

Nutrition labels

GOAL ➤ Interpret nutrition information

MyPyramid
STEPS TO A HEALTHIER YOU
MyPyramid.gov

| GRAINS | VEGETABLES | FRUITS | MILK | MEAT & BEANS |

GRAINS Make half your grains whole	VEGETABLES Vary your veggies	FRUITS Focus on fruits	MILK Get your calcium-rich foods	MEAT & BEANS Go lean with protein
Eat at least 3 oz. of whole-grain cereals, breads, crackers, rice, or pasta every day 1 oz. is about 1 slice of bread, about 1 cup of breakfast cereal, or ½ cup of cooked rice, cereal, or pasta	Eat more dark-green veggies like broccoli, spinach, and other dark leafy greens Eat more orange vegetables like carrots and sweet potatoes Eat more dry beans and peas like pinto beans, kidney beans, and lentils	Eat a variety of fruit Choose fresh, frozen, canned, or dried fruit Go easy on fruit juices	Go low-fat or fat-free when you choose milk, yogurt, and other milk products If you don't or can't consume milk, choose lactose-free products or other calcium sources such as fortified foods and beverages	Choose low-fat or lean meats and poultry Bake it, broil it, or grill it Vary your protein routine — choose more fish, beans, peas, nuts, and seeds
For a 2,000-calorie diet, you need the amounts below from each food group. To find the amounts that are right for you, go to MyPyramid.gov.				
Eat 6 oz. every day	Eat 2½ cups every day	Eat 2 cups every day	Get 3 cups every day; for kids aged 2 to 8, it's 2	Eat 5½ oz. every day

 A The food pyramid can help you make good decisions about daily food choices.
It tells you how much of each food group you should eat every day.
Skim the information in the pyramid and answer the questions below.

1. Which foods should you eat the most of? _____

2. Which foods should you eat the least of? _____

3. How much fruit should you eat every day? _____

4. What food group is rice in? _____

5. What is an example of an orange vegetable? _____

GOAL ➤ Interpret nutrition information

B Read the tips for healthy eating. Put a check mark (✓) next to the tips you follow or would like to follow. Then, discuss your answers with a partner.

Tips for healthy eating	Follow	Would like to follow
1. Keep raw vegetables in the refrigerator to eat as a snack.		
2. Eat a variety of foods to get all the nutrients you need.		
3. Eat lean meats like fish and chicken.		
4. Choose fat-free or low-fat dairy products.		
5. Try not to drink beverages with a lot of sugar such as soft drinks.		
6. Flavor foods with herbs and spices instead of salt.		
7. Pay attention to serving sizes.		
8. Choose foods that have less saturated fat.		

C Reading nutrition labels can help you make smart eating choices. Read the nutrition label for macaroni and cheese.

Macaroni & Cheese Nutrition Facts	
Amount Per Serving	
Calories 250	Calories from Fat 110
	% Daily Value*
Total Fat 12g	**18%**
Saturated Fat 3g	**15%**
Cholesterol 30mg	**10%**
Sodium 470mg	**20%**
Total Carbohydrate 31g	**10%**
Dietary Fiber 0g	**0%**
Sugars 5g	
Protein 5g	
Vitamin A	**4%**
Vitamin C	**2%**
Calcium	**20%**
Iron	**4%**

*Percent Daily Values are based on a 2,000 calorie diet. Your Daily Values may be higher or lower depending on your calorie needs.

D Listen to Darla explain nutritional information to her grandmother.

CD 1
TR 12

E Listen to each part of the conversation again and answer the questions below. Fill in the circle next to the correct answer.

Part 1

1. What does Grandma need to look at if she wants to watch her salt intake?
   ○ sodium   ○ saturated fat

2. How many servings are in this box of macaroni and cheese?
   ○ two   ○ four

3. How many calories should an average adult have each day?
   ○ 200   ○ 2,000

Part 2

1. What should Grandma avoid to have a healthy heart?
   ○ cholesterol and saturated fat
   ○ carbohydrates and saturated fat

2. What should a diabetic look for on a food label?
   ○ sugar   ○ salt

3. What nutrient helps digestion?
   ○ iron   ○ fiber

4. What nutrient is good for bones?
   ○ calcium   ○ vitamin A

F Read the nutritional guidelines.

> **Recommended Amount of Calories and Fat Per Day**
> - 2,000 calories per day
> - 20 or less grams saturated fat
> - 65 grams total fat
>
> **Quick Guide to % Daily Value* for Nutrients**
> 5% or less is LOW   20% or more is HIGH
>
> *Percent Daily Values are based on a 2,000-calorie diet. Your Daily Values may be higher or lower depending on your calorie needs.

G Now look at the macaroni and cheese label on page 91. Answer the questions below.

1. Is macaroni and cheese high in fat? _____

2. Is macaroni and cheese low in sodium? _____

3. Does it contain any protein? How much? _____

4. What vitamins does it contain? Is it high in vitamins? _____

5. Is macaroni and cheese a good source of calcium? _____

6. Do you think macaroni and cheese is a healthy food choice? Why or why not?

_____

H Work with a partner and plan three meals based on the food pyramid on page 90. Share your plan with your class. Whose menu is the most delicious and nutritious?

Healthy living

GOAL ➤ Interpret fitness information

A You are going to read part of an article about physical fitness. Before you read, write one piece of advice that you think the article will contain. Then, read the article.

Be Physically Active Each Day

Being physically active and maintaining a healthy weight are necessary for good health. Children, teens, adults, and the elderly can improve their health by including moderate physical activity in their daily lives.

Try to get at least 30 minutes (adults) or 60 minutes (children) of moderate physical activity most days of the week, preferably daily. No matter what activity you choose, you can do it all at once, or spread it out over the day.

Make Physical Activity a Regular Part of Your Routine

Choose activities that you enjoy and that you can do regularly. Some people prefer activities that fit into their daily routine, like gardening or taking extra trips up and down stairs. Others prefer a regular exercise program, such as a physical activity program at their worksite. Some do both. The important thing is to be physically active every day.

Adapted from: Dietary Guidelines for Americans 2000 Center for Nutritional Policy and Promotion, USDA.

B Decide if the statements are true or false. Bubble in the correct answers.

	True	False
1. Physical exercise is necessary for good health.	○	○
2. Elderly people do not need to exercise.	○	○
3. Adults should exercise every day.	○	○
4. It is better to exercise throughout the day.	○	○
5. Climbing stairs is a good way to exercise regularly.	○	○
6. The most important thing is to exercise regularly.	○	○

C Discuss these questions with your partner.

1. Do you exercise more or less than recommended in the article? _____

2. Does your workplace offer physical activity programs? What are they? _____

_____

D Look at the examples of physical activities. Which is an example of a routine activity? Which is an example of a recreational activity?

Ana plays tennis
twice a week
with her friend.

Mike rides his bicycle
to the office every day.

E Read the list of routine activities. Put a check mark (✓) next to the activities you have tried. Put an *X* next to the activities you would like to try. Add two more activities.

❒ Walk or ride a bike to work.
❒ Walk up stairs instead of taking an elevator.
❒ Get off the bus a few stops early and walk the remaining distance.
❒ Garden.
❒ Push a stroller.

❒ Clean the house.
❒ Play actively with children.
❒ Take a brisk ten-minute walk or bike ride in the morning, at lunch, and after dinner.
❒ _____
❒ _____

F Read the list of recreational activities. Put a check mark (✓) next to the activities you have tried. Put an *X* next to the activities you would like to try. Add two more activities.

❒ Walk, jog, or bicycle.
❒ Swim or do water aerobics.
❒ Play tennis or racquetball.
❒ Golf (pull cart or carry clubs).
❒ Canoe.
❒ Cross-country ski.

❒ Play basketball.
❒ Dance.
❒ Take part in an exercise program at work, home, school, or gym.
❒ _____
❒ _____

LESSON **5** **GOAL** ➤ Interpret fitness information

G Read the paragraph. Then, discuss the questions below with a partner.

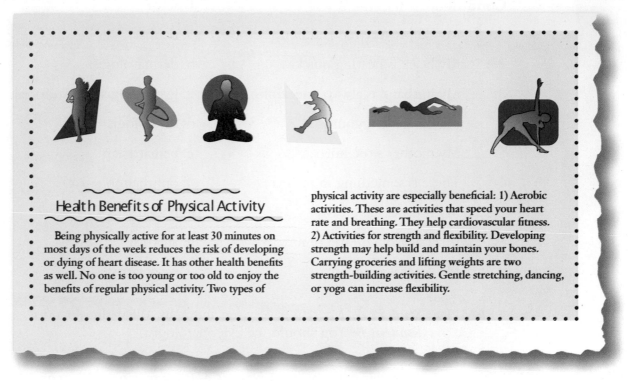

Health Benefits of Physical Activity

Being physically active for at least 30 minutes on most days of the week reduces the risk of developing or dying of heart disease. It has other health benefits as well. No one is too young or too old to enjoy the benefits of regular physical activity. Two types of physical activity are especially beneficial: 1) Aerobic activities. These are activities that speed your heart rate and breathing. They help cardiovascular fitness. 2) Activities for strength and flexibility. Developing strength may help build and maintain your bones. Carrying groceries and lifting weights are two strength-building activities. Gentle stretching, dancing, or yoga can increase flexibility.

1. Why are aerobic activities good for you?
2. What are some examples of aerobic activities?
3. Why are activities for strength good for your bones?
4. What are some examples of strength-building activities?
5. What types of activities can increase your flexibility?
6. What are some activities you do for strength and flexibility?

H Read about more benefits of physical activity. Then, discuss the questions with a partner.

More Health Benefits of Physical Activity

➤ Increases physical fitness

➤ Helps build and maintain healthy bones, muscles, and joints

➤ Builds endurance and muscular strength

➤ Helps manage weight

➤ Lowers risk factors for cardiovascular disease, colon cancer, and type 2 diabetes

➤ Helps control blood pressure

➤ Promotes psychological well-being and self-esteem

➤ Reduces feelings of depression and anxiety

1. What diseases can exercise help prevent?
2. How does exercise help your circulatory system?
3. How does exercise affect your mood and your mental health?
4. What are some other benefits of exercise?

Review

A **Match each condition with the doctor who treats it. Then, use this information to practice the conversation below with a partner.**

Condition	Doctor
1. _b_ My skin is very red and itchy.	a. dentist
2. ___ My heart is beating quickly.	b. dermatologist
3. ___ My husband is always sneezing.	c. gynecologist/obstetrician
4. ___ My baby is coughing.	d. cardiologist
5. ___ My mother's toe hurts.	e. pediatrician
6. ___ There is something in my eye.	f. ophthalmologist
7. ___ My brother has a cavity.	g. podiatrist
8. ___ I feel nervous all the time.	h. allergist
9. ___ My sister is pregnant.	i. psychiatrist

EXAMPLE: *Student A:* <u>My skin is very red and itchy</u>. What should I do?
             Student B: You should see a <u>dermatologist</u>.

B **Make sentences using the present perfect and *for* or *since*. (*Lesson 2*)**

1. Ali has a backache / Monday

   <u>Ali has had a backache since Monday.</u>

2. my neck hurts / two days

_____

3. Maria feels dizzy / yesterday

_____

4. my children have a cold / Friday

_____

5. Peter is sick / two weeks

_____

6. I have an earache / 10:00 A.M.

_____

7. they are absent from work / one month

_____

C Complete the sentences with a future conditional verb.

1. If you eat out every night, _you will spend a lot of money._

2. _____ if he goes to the best doctors in the country.

3. If _____, they will look and feel great.

4. If Paulo smokes a pack of cigarettes a day, _____.

5. If _____, you will get sick.

6. If _____, you will improve your flexibility.

7. If you read nutritional labels, _____.

8. If _____, you will have a lot of cavities.

D Read the information. Then, decide if the statements below are true or false. Bubble in the correct answer.

Find your balance between food and physical activity

- Be sure to stay within your daily calorie needs.
- Be physically active for at least 30 minutes most days of the week.
- About 60 minutes a day of physical activity may be needed to prevent weight gain.
- For sustaining weight loss, at least 60 to 90 minutes a day of physical activity may be required.
- Children and teenagers should be physically active for 60 minutes every day, or most days.

Know the limits on fats, sugars, and salt (sodium)

- Make most of your fat sources from fish, nuts, and vegetable oils.
- Limit solid fats like butter, stick margarine, shortening, and lard, as well as foods that contain these.
- Check the Nutrition Facts label to keep saturated fats, *trans* fats, and sodium low.
- Choose food and beverages low in added sugars. Added sugars contribute calories with few, if any, nutrients.

	True	False
1. Children only need to exercise for 20 minutes a day.	○	○
2. Choose foods that are low in added sugar.	○	○
3. If you want to lose weight, you should exercise between 60 and 90 minutes a day.	○	○
4. Fish and nuts are good fats.	○	○

E With a partner, ask and answer questions about the nutritional information on the package of frozen peas. Decide if the frozen peas are a healthy choice. (Lesson 4)

Frozen Peas Nutrition Facts	Amount/Serving	%DV*
Ingredients: green peas, salt Serving size 2/3 cup (88g) Servings Per Container About 5	**Total Carbohydrate** 12g	4%
	Fiber 4g	16%
	Sugars 6g	
Calories 70	**Protein** 5g	
Calories from Fat 5	**Vitamin A**	6%
Total Fat 0.5g 1%	**Vitamin C**	15%
Sat. Fat 0g 0%	**Calcium** 0%	0%
Cholesterol 0mg 0%	**Iron** 4%	4%
Sodium 100mg 4%	*Percent Daily Values are based on a 2,000 calorie diet. Your Daily Values may be higher or lower depending on your calorie needs.	

Home Style
Frozen Peas

1. Are the peas high in fat?
2. Are the peas low in sodium?
3. Do they contain any protein? How much?
4. What vitamins do they contain? Are they high in vitamins?
5. Are the peas a good source of calcium?
6. Do you think peas are a healthy food choice?

F Look back at the articles on pages 93 and 95. Write four pieces of advice that you would like to follow. (Lesson 5)

1. _____
2. _____
3. _____
4. _____

My Dictionary

If you want to use a new word, it's important to know what part of speech it is. Is it a person, place, or thing (a noun); an action (a verb); or a word that describes a noun (an adjective)?

Look at the words from Unit 5 in the box below. Make a chart like the one below. Put each word into the correct category in the chart. Use a dictionary to check your answers.

ankle	ophthalmologist	dentist	worry	itchy	sore	cavity
stay	hospital	tired	cough	diabetes	stress	protect	gain
raw	cholesterol	healthy	active	maintain	gentle	stretch

NOUN	VERB	ADJECTIVE
ophthalmologist	worry	itchy

Learner Log

In this unit, you learned many things about health. How comfortable do you feel doing each of the skills listed below? Rate your comfort level on a scale of 1 to 4.

1 = Need more practice   **2** = OK   **3** = Good   **4** = Great!

Life Skill	Comfort Level	Page
I can identify parts of the body.	1 2 3 4	_____
I can identify doctors and their specializations.	1 2 3 4	_____
I can communicate my symptoms to a doctor.	1 2 3 4	_____
I can interpret food labels.	1 2 3 4	_____
I can identify healthy and unhealthy habits.	1 2 3 4	_____
I can interpret information on dietary guidelines.	1 2 3 4	_____
I can interpret information on fitness.	1 2 3 4	_____

If you circled 1 or 2, write down the page number where you can review this skill.

Reflection

1. What was the most useful skill you learned in this unit? _____

2. How will this help you in life? _____

Team Project

BE PHYSICALLY ACTIVE EACH DAY

Create a healthy living plan.

You are a team of doctors and health-care professionals who have decided to make a healthy living plan to give patients when they leave the hospital.

1. Form a team with four or five students. Choose a position for each member of your team.

POSITION	JOB DESCRIPTION	STUDENT NAME
Student 1: Health Advisor	See that everyone speaks English. See that everyone participates.	
Student 2: Writer	Write down information for plan.	
Student 3: Designer	Design plan layout and add artwork.	
Students 4/5: Health Representatives	Help writer and designer with their work.	

2. Make a list of all the information you want to include in your plan (healthy habits, fitness and nutrition advice, etc.). (Lessons 3–5)

3. Create the different sections of your plan, for example, a guide to reading nutritional labels, a guide to exercise, a list of doctors and their specializations, and a guide to common symptoms and diseases. (Lessons 1–5)

4. Add artwork to the plan, for example, maps of parks and gyms in your area or a drawing of the food pyramid.

5. Make a collage of all your information.

6. Share your healthy living plan with the class.

UNIT 6 Getting Hired

GOALS

➤ Identify job titles and skills
➤ Identify job skills and preferences
➤ Interpret job advertisements
➤ Fill out a job application
➤ Interview for a job

LESSON **1** Jobs and careers

GOAL ➤ Identify job titles and skills

Vocabulary   Grammar
Life Skills
Academic   Pronunciation

(A) Look at the picures and write the correct letter next to each job title below.

a.

c.

b.

d.

__c__ 1. graphic artist

____ 2. dental hygienist

____ 3. home health-care aide

____ 4. bookkeeper

(B) Talk to your partner about the four jobs. Which job is the most interesting? Which job is the most difficult? Why?

C **Match the job with the description.**

___ 1. graphic artist	a. cleans teeth
___ 2. repair technician	b. takes care of children
___ 3. administrative assistant	c. designs and maintains yards
___ 4. dental hygienist	d. writes programs for computers
___ 5. landscaper	e. designs artwork for companies
___ 6. bookkeeper	f. types, files, and does general office work
___ 7. home health-care aide	g. uses equipment in a factory or on a construction site
___ 8. computer programmer	h. keeps financial records
___ 9. nanny	i. fixes appliances and equipment
___ 10. machine operator	j. takes care of sick people in their own homes

D **Look at the pictures below. What do you think each person does? Write a job title from the box below each picture.**

cashier	custodian	doctor	electrician	food server	judge
lawyer	nurse	plumber	scientist	~~teacher~~	postal worker

1. ___teacher___

2. _____

3. _____

4. _____

5. _____

6. _____

7. _____

8. _____

LESSON 1

GOAL ➤ **Identify job titles and skills**

E Work with a small group to write one skill for each job title below.

Job title   Skill

1. custodian   _____

2. teacher   _____

3. doctor   _____

4. food server   _____

5. judge   _____

6. nurse   _____

F Work with a small group to write the job title for each skill below. (*Hint*: The job titles are from Exercise D.)

Job title   Skill

1. _____   fixes leaking pipes

2. _____   delivers mail and packages

3. _____   fixes electrical problems

4. _____   rings up the total for purchased items

5. _____   defends crime victims

6. _____   invents new medicine

G Practice the conversation with a partner. Use the job titles and skills from this lesson.

EXAMPLE: *Student A:* What does <u>a graphic artist</u> do?
               Student B: <u>A graphic artist designs artwork for companies.</u>

H Work with a partner. Think of four more jobs and write what each person does.

EXAMPLE: <u>A farmer grows fruits and vegetables.</u>

1. _____

2. _____

3. _____

4. _____

LESSON 2

What can you do?

GOAL ➤ Identify job skills and preferences

Vocabulary   Grammar
Life Skills
Academic   Pronunciation

A What are your special job skills? Put a check mark (✓) next to the things you are good at. Add two skills to the list.

❑ answer phones and take messages
❑ assemble things
❑ cook
❑ draw
❑ drive a car or truck
❑ fix machines
❑ order supplies
❑ balance accounts
❑ operate machines
❑ talk to customers
❑ read maps
❑ sew
❑ speak other languages
❑ take care of children
❑ take care of the elderly
❑ type
❑ repair computers
❑ use computers

❑ _____

❑ _____

B Are there any skills you want to improve? Are there any skills you want to learn? List them below.

Improve: _____

Learn: _____

C Exchange your list with a partner. Think of ways your partner can learn or improve the skills he or she wrote down. Use ideas from the box below.

volunteer	ask a friend to teach you	practice at home
take a class	find a job training program	get trained at your company

EXAMPLE: *Student A:*   I want to learn to <u>take care of the elderly</u>.
                    Student B: Maybe you can <u>volunteer at a hospital or nursing home</u>.

GOAL ➤ **Identify job skills and preferences**

D Claude needs a job. Can you suggest a good job for him?

Claude is quiet and shy. He is friendly, but he doesn't really like to talk to customers. He is very good at assembling things. When he was a teenager, he enjoyed fixing bicycles. He likes to be busy. He wants to get a job where he can use his technical skills.

E Study the chart with your classmates and teacher. Then, underline examples of infinitives and gerunds in the paragraph above.

Infinitives and Gerunds Infinitive = *to* + verb Gerund = verb + *ing*			
Verb	**Infinitive or Gerund?**	**Example sentence**	**Other verbs that follow the same rule**
want	infinitive	He wants *to get* a job.	plan, decide
enjoy	gerund	He enjoys *fixing* bicycles.	finish, give up
like	both	He likes *to talk*. He likes *talking*.	love, hate

F Are these verbs followed by an infinitive, a gerund, or both? Fill in the circle next to the correct answer.

	Infinitive	Gerund	Both
1. I like _____ on a team.	○ to work	○ working	● to work/working
2. I enjoy _____ problems.	○ to solve	○ solving	○ to solve/solving
3. I want _____ to customers.	○ to talk	○ talking	○ to talk/talking
4. I decided _____ math.	○ to study	○ studying	○ to study/studying
5. I hate _____ decisions.	○ to make	○ making	○ to make/making
6. I gave up _____ two years ago.	○ to smoke	○ smoking	○ to smoke/smoking
7. I love _____ machines.	○ to repair	○ repairing	○ to repair/repairing

GOAL ➤ **Identify job skills and preferences**

G What are your special job skills? Put a check mark (✓) next to the things you are good at. Add two skills to the list.

- ❑ solve problems
- ❑ work under pressure
- ❑ work in a fast-paced environment
- ❑ work on a team
- ❑ make decisions
- ❑ pay attention to details
- ❑ work with my hands
- ❑ read and follow directions

- ❑ help people
- ❑ organize information
- ❑ work with money
- ❑ talk to customers
- ❑ _____
- ❑ _____

H Study the chart with your classmates and teacher.

Gerunds and Nouns after Prepositions					
Subject	Verb	Adjective	Preposition	Gerund/Noun	Example sentence
I	am	good	at	calculating	I am good at *calculating*.
she	is	good	at	math	She is good at *math*.
A gerund or a noun follows an adjective + a preposition. Some other examples of adjectives + prepositions are *interested in, afraid of, tired of, bad at,* and *worried about*.					

I Tell your partner about your skills and interests. What things are you *good at*, *bad at*, *interested in*, *tired of*, and *afraid of*? Your partner will suggest a good job for you.

EXAMPLE: *Student A*: I am good at paying attention to details. I'm interested in organizing information.
Student B: Maybe you should be a bookkeeper.

J Write a paragraph about your job skills on a piece of paper. What are you good at? What are you interested in learning? How do you plan to learn or practice these skills?

LESSON 3

Help wanted

GOAL ➤ Interpret job advertisements

A Read the following job advertisements.

24 NewsObserver   Sunday, October I

HELP WANTED

① Auto technician: Do you like to work on cars? Do you have an excellent attitude, good mechanical skills, & the ability to learn fast? Strong electronics background preferred. Call Chrissy at (310) 555-9078.

④ Photographer. Reliable? Enjoy children? Join our team taking school pictures. A cheerful personality is a plus. We offer paid training. Must have car & proof of insurance. Fax resume to Lifetouch Studios 318-555-7440.

⑦ Need caring, **Licensed Nurse's Aide** to care for elderly couple. Housing on site. Competitive salary. Send resume with references to: P.O. Box 2728 Morgan City, LA 70381.

② Acme Construction, **Administrative Assistant.** Min. 2 yrs. exp in clerical. Good computer skills req. Ability to work under pressure and type 40 wpm. Fax res. 818-555-3141.

⑤ Fast-growing supermarket chain seeks bright, motivated **managers** for meat & produce. Prior management experience, required. Excellent salary and benefits. Fax resume to: 626-555-1342.

⑧ Dependable **custodian** for 3 apartment buildings. Min. 2 yrs exp. plumbing, carpentry, painting, repair. Must have own tools and car $12-14/hr+benes 818-555-3500x523.

③ Receptionist, weekends: 10am-6pm. Requires HS diploma (or equiv) and 1 year experience. Excellent phone & organizational skills along with a pleasant attitude a must! Please apply in person to: 396 Marcasel Avenue, Los Angeles, CA 90066.

⑥ Detail-oriented **pharmacy clerk** needed to process insurance forms & assist customer. Must be biling/Spanish. Strong commun & org skills. Great bene. Call: Armine (605) 555-6613

WA

B Are there any words or abbreviations that are new to you? List them below and discuss them with your classmates and teacher.

_____ _____ _____

_____ _____ _____

_____ _____ _____

GOAL ➤ Interpret job advertisements

C Read the ads in Exercise A again and answer the questions below.

1. What experience should the auto technician have? <u>electronics background</u>

2. Which employer wants someone who can work under pressure? _____

3. Which job provides training? _____

4. Which job requires references? _____

5. Which jobs require a friendly personality? _____

6. Which jobs require a car? _____

7. Which jobs require someone who likes details? _____

8. Which job requires someone who is bilingual? _____

9. Which job offers housing? _____

10. What are ways to apply for these jobs? _____

D What skills are required for each job advertised in Exercise A? Complete the chart.

Job	Skills required or preferred
1. Photographer	_____ _____
2. Custodian	_____ _____
3. Pharmacy clerk	_____ _____
4. Auto technician	_____ _____
5. Receptionist	_____ _____
6. Manager	_____ _____

 LESSON 3

GOAL ➤ Interpret job advertisements

E Read the descriptions and decide which job or jobs from page 107 each person should apply for. Write the job titles.

1. Lance recently moved here and needs to find a job. At his old job, he answered the phone, typed letters, and filed paperwork. He would like a job doing the same thing. What jobs should he apply for?

   _____

2. Kyung was recently laid off from his janitorial job at the local school district. He had been working there for ten years and took care of all the maintenance and repairs for the school. What job should he apply for?

   _____

3. Kim has two kids and wants to work while they are in school. She doesn't have any clerical skills, but she is cheerful and friendly. What job should she apply for?

   _____

4. Rita manages a bakery but wants to find a job closer to home. She is smart and willing to work hard. She really likes to work with people and would like to find a job in the same line of work. What job should she apply for?

   _____

F Answer the following questions about yourself.

1. Which job advertised on page 107 would you be best at? Why?

   _____

2. Which job would you most like to have? Why?

   _____

3. Which job would you like the least? Why?

   _____

G Write an ad for your dream job. Include the job title, skills, preferences, pay, and any other necessary information.

```



```

GOAL ➤ Fill out a job application

A Look at the ways people apply for jobs. How did you get your last job? What's the best way to get a job? Discuss your answers with a partner.

➤ personal connection (you know someone at the company)

➤ go to an employment agency

➤ reply to a classified ad

➤ see a *Help Wanted* sign and fill out an application

➤ introduce yourself to the manager and fill out an application

➤ send a resume to a company

B Not every business advertises available positions. If you want to work somewhere, you should go in and ask for an application. Read the conversation below.

Ramona: Excuse me. May I speak to the manager, please?
Employee: She's not here right now. Can I help you?
Ramona: Are you hiring now?
Employee: As a matter of fact, we are.
Ramona: What positions are you hiring for?
Employee: We need a <u>manicurist</u> and a <u>receptionist</u>.
Ramona: Great. Can I have an application, please?
Employee: Here you go. You can drop it off any time.
Ramona: Thanks a lot.
Employee: Sure. Good luck.

C Practice the conversation above. Fill in your own job titles.

D On a job application, you have to fill out certain information. Match the type of information to its description.

_c_ 1. Personal Information   a. people that can be called who know you

___ 2. Employment History   b. previous jobs you had

___ 3. Availability   c. name, address, special skills

___ 4. Education   d. schools you attended

___ 5. References   e. when you are free to work

E Look at Ramona's job application. Discuss the sections with your classmates and teacher.

JOB APPLICATION

Position Applied for: Manicurist   Interviewed by _____

PERSONAL INFORMATION

Name Jimenez   Ramona   **Phone** (714) 555-9765__
          last   first   mi

Last Five Year Employment History (Please list most recent positions first)

Employer (company, address)	Position	Dates		Reason for Leaving
		from	to	
Jardin Nails 8976 Flower Lane Garden Grove, CA 92842	manicurist	1/05	3/07	salon closed

AVAILABILLITY

Write an "x" if available

	Sun	Mon	Tue	Wed	Thu	Fri	Sat
Morning	X	X	X	X		X	X
Afternoon	X	X	X	X		X	X
Evening							

EDUCATION	School and Address	Course of Study	Number of Years Completed	Degree or Diploma
Elementary School	Escuela do los Arboles Mexico	Basic skills	8 years	certificate of completion
High School	Garden Grove High School 11271 Stanford Ave., Garden Grove, CA 92840	general education	2 years	none

REFERENCES	Name	Position	Company	Telephone
	Kim Nguyen	Manager	Jardin Nails	(714) 555-3635

  F Read the rules for filling out an application below. What words could go in the blanks? Now, listen and fill in the missing words.

CD 1
TR 13

Rules for Filling Out an Application

1. Use a dark _____, blue or _____ ink.

2. Don't _____ any mistakes. Use correction fluid to _____ any mistakes.

3. Answer every _____. If the question doesn't apply to you, write _____ (Not Applicable).

4. Tell the _____! Never _____ on your job application.

5. Don't _____ or wrinkle the application.

6. Keep the application _____ no food or coffee stains!

7. Write as _____ as possible. _____ it if you can.

8. If you don't _____ the question, ask someone before you answer it.

G Fill out the job application with your own information.

JOB APPLICATION

Date _____

Position Applied for: _____   Interviewed by _____

PERSONAL INFORMATION

Name _____   Phone ( ) _____
        last   first   mi

Present Address _____

City _____ State _____ Zip _____

Special Skills _____

Type WPM _____ Languages _____

Computer Skills _____

Last Five Years Employment History (Please list most recent positions first)

Employer (company, address)	Position	Dates from	Dates to	Reason for Leaving

---

AVAILABILITY

		Sun	Mon	Tue	Wed	Thu	Fri	Sat
Write an "x" if available	Morning							
	Afternoon							
	Evening							

EDUCATION

	School and Address	Course of Study	Number of Years Completed	Degree or Diploma
Elementary School				
High School				
College(s)				
Other				

REFERENCES

Name	Position	Company	Telephone

I certify that the above information is true to the best of my knowledge. I authorize previous employers to provide any information they feel appropriate.

Signature _____

Why do you want to work here?

GOAL ➤ Interview for a job

A Have you ever had a job interview? What happened? Tell your partner.

B During a job interview, an employer will try to find out about an applicant's character and personality. Read and listen to find out what interviewers look for during an interview.

CD 1
TR 14

> Your job interview is the most important part of the application process. This is when the employer gets to meet you and learn more about you. Employers are interested in your skills and experience, but they also look for personality and character traits.
>
> **Do you stand tall and smile confidently?** Employers will notice your self-confidence. Managers want to hire employees who have confidence in themselves and will have confidence in the job they are doing.
>
> **Do you like to work hard and do a good job?** Another important thing an interviewer looks for is enthusiasm about work. People who are enthusiastic about a job make great employees. They are happy with the work and usually stay with the company for a while.
>
> **Are you friendly and easy to talk to?** Do you pay attention to how other people are feeling? Warmth and sensitivity are also very important traits. A person with these characteristics will make a good coworker, someone who can work well with others.
>
> Do you have some or all of these traits? Can you show that you have these traits in an interview? If the answer is yes, you will have a good chance of getting the job.

C Discuss the following questions with a partner.

1. In your opinion, which is the most important trait: self-confidence, enthusiasm, or a friendly personality?

2. According to the reading, how can you use body language to show you are self-confident? Can you think of any other ways you can show confidence through body language?

3. How can you show an employer that you are enthusiastic about the job and the company?

4. According to the article, why do employers like to hire warm, sensitive people?

5. Do you think there are other character traits that employers like? What are they?

D Imagine you are interviewing someone for a job as an administrative assistant in a busy doctor's office. List six character traits you would look for. Use ideas from the box or your own.

honest	confident	funny	friendly	sensitive	thoughtful	enthusiastic
arrogant	motivated	warm	helpful	careful	intelligent	sneaky

1. _____   3. _____   5. _____

2. _____   4. _____   6. _____

E With your classmates, discuss what kind of clothing and accessories are appropriate or not appropriate for a job interview. Fill in the chart. Use the words from the box and add some of your own ideas.

earrings

tattoos

makeup

sneakers

tie

pants

suit

belt

shorts

cuff links

dress

handbag

briefcase

jacket

t-shirt

long hair

jeans

nail polish

jewelry

Men	Appropriate	Not appropriate
	long-sleeved shirt	T-shirt

Women	Appropriate	Not appropriate

 F Study the chart with your classmates and teacher.

Would rather					
Subject	*would rather*	**Base form**	*than*	**Base form**	**Example sentence**
I, you, she, he, it, we, they	would ('d) rather	work alone	than	work with people	I would rather work alone than work with people.
Note: You can omit the second verb if it is the same as the first verb. **Example:** I would rather work nights than (work) days.					

G Which work situation do you prefer? Talk to your partner about your preferences.

EXAMPLE: *Student A:* Would you rather work inside or outside?
            Student B: I'd rather work inside because I hate the cold.

1. work alone / on a team
2. work days / nights
3. get paid hourly / weekly
4. have your own business / work for someone else
5. retire at 65 / work until you are 70
6. have a male boss / a female boss

 H Write two sentences about your ideal work situation.

EXAMPLE: I'd rather work on a team than alone because I like talking to people.

1. _____

2. _____

I Imagine you are preparing for a job interview. Choose a job from the ads on page 107 or one of your own. Work with a partner and answer the questions below.

1. What are your skills? _____

2. Why do you think you would be good at this job? _____

3. How would you describe your personality? _____

4. What did you like and dislike about your last job? _____

5. Would you rather work full time or part time? _____

6. What salary do you expect? _____

Review

A Read each skill below and write a job title on the line. (Lesson 1)

1. cleans teeth _____

2. types, files, and does general office work _____

3. takes a patient's temperature and blood pressure _____

4. fixes pipes _____

5. cleans office buildings _____

6. operates machinery _____

7. takes care of children _____

8. maintains yards _____

B List six job skills you have. (Lesson 2)

1. _____

2. _____

3. _____

4. _____

5. _____

6. _____

C Complete these sentences using a gerund or an infinitive form of the verb in parentheses. (Lesson 2)

1. I like _____ on a team. (work)

2. I am good at _____ to customers. (talk)

3. They hate _____ the phone. (answer)

4. I decided _____ computers next semester. (study)

5. He is interested in _____ cars. (repair)

6. We finished _____ our reports yesterday. (write)

D Read the job ads. (Lesson 3)

1. Administrative Assistant, weekdays: 10 A.M.- 6 P.M. Requires HS diploma and 1 year experience. **Excellent phone & organizational skills** along with a pleasant attitude a must! Please apply in person to: 7790 Maribel Avenue, Los Angeles, CA 90066.

2. Fast-growing supermarket chain is looking for personable, motivated **cashiers**. Must be good with numbers. **Excellent salary and benefits.** Fax resume to: 626-555-8879

3. Reliable **custodian** for local school district. Min 1 yr exp. **cleaning, plumbing, carpentry, painting, repair.** Will provide supplies and tools. $12-14/hr + benefits. Call 818-555-6879.

E Write the correct job title(s) on the line: *administrative assistant, cashier,* or *custodian.*

1. For which job do you have to be good with numbers? _____

2. Which jobs require experience? _____

3. Which job requires a high school diploma? _____

4. Which job requires a resume? _____

5. Which jobs offer benefits? _____

6. Personality is NOT important for which job? _____

F Fill out the partial job application. (Lesson 4)

JOB APPLICATION

Position Applied for: _____   Date _____   Interviewed by _____

PERSONAL INFORMATION

Name _____   Phone ( )
　　　last　　　first　　　mi

Special Skills _____

Last Five Years Employment History (Please list most recent positions first)

Employer (company, address)	Position	Dates		Reason for Leaving
		from	to	

AVAILABILITY

Write an "x" if available		Sun	Mon	Tue	Wed	Thu	Fri	Sat
	Morning							
	Afternoon							
	Evening							

EDUCATION

	School and Address	Course of Study	Number of Years Completed	Degree or Diploma
Elementary School				
High School				

REFERENCES

Name	Position	Company	Telephone

Review

G What would you rather do? Think about the things you don't like about your current job. Write four sentences using *would rather* to express your preferences. (Lesson 5)

1. _____
2. _____
3. _____
4. _____

H What kind of personality should people have for these jobs? Write two adjectives for each job. Share your answers with a partner. (Lesson 5)

1. home health-care aide: <u>responsible, caring</u> _____

2. manager in a clothing store: _____

3. receptionist in a dentist's office: _____

4. nanny: _____

5. custodian in a school: _____

6. teacher: _____

I Write six interview questions for one of the following jobs. Interview a partner. (Lesson 5)

landscaper	receptionist	furniture store manager	computer technician
bookkeeper	waiter	assembler in a factory	home health-care aide

EXAMPLE: receptionist <u>Can you type?</u> _____

1. _____
2. _____
3. _____
4. _____
5. _____
6. _____

My Dictionary

Word Stress

Your dictionary will tell you where to put the stress in each word. Dictionaries use different symbols to show stress. What symbol does your dictionary use?

EXAMPLE: 'ap-ple (The stress is on the first syllable.)

Look up the following words in the dictionary. Write them with the correct syllable stress.

1. applicant <u>'ap-pli-cant</u>

2. previous _____

3. bookkeeper _____

4. technician _____

5. computer _____

6. equipment _____

7. environment _____

8. require _____

Now practice saying the words, using the correct stress.

Learner Log

In this unit, you learned many things about getting hired. How comfortable do you feel doing each of the skills listed below? Rate your comfort level on a scale of 1 to 4.

1 = Need more practice   **2** = OK   **3** = Good   **4** = Great!

Life Skill	Comfort Level	Page
I can identify job titles and skills.	1 2 3 4	_____
I can describe my job skills.	1 2 3 4	_____
I can interpret job advertisements.	1 2 3 4	_____
I can fill out a job application.	1 2 3 4	_____
I know what is appropriate to wear to an interview.	1 2 3 4	_____
I am familiar with interview questions.	1 2 3 4	_____

If you circled 1 or 2, write down the page number where you can review this skill.

Reflection

1. What was the most useful skill you learned in this unit?_____

_____

2. How will this help you in life? _____

Team Project

Create a job application portfolio.

With your team, you will plan the contents and layout for a job application portfolio. Each student will create his or her own job application portfolio.

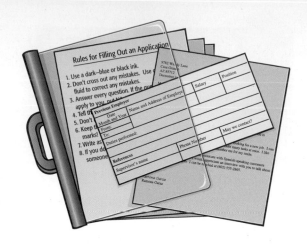

What does a job application portfolio include?

➤ a job application information sheet
➤ a list of rules for filling out a job application
➤ a list of skills
➤ sample interview questions and answers
➤ certificates

➤ awards
➤ transcripts
➤ performance reviews
➤ letters of recommendation

---

1. Form a team with four or five students. Choose a position for each member of your team.

POSITION	JOB DESCRIPTION	STUDENT NAME
Student 1: Leader	See that everyone speaks English and participates.	
Student 2: Secretary	Write list for job application portfolio.	
Student 3: Designer	Design order of job application portfolio.	
Students 4/5: Member(s)	Help secretary and designer with their work.	

2. Make a list of all the information you want to include in your portfolio. Look at the list above for help. Decide how many pages you will need.

3. With your team, decide the best order for your portfolio.

4. Collect and create items to put in your individual portfolio. Put your portfolio together.

5. Share your portfolio with at least two other students.

6. Set up an interview with your teacher and share your portfolio with him or her.

On the Job

GOALS

➤ **Compare employee behavior and attitudes**

➤ **Interpret a pay stub**

➤ **Interpret benefit information**

➤ **Identify safe workplace behavior**

➤ **Communicate at work**

LESSON 1

Attitudes at work

GOAL ➤ Compare employee behavior and attitudes

A Listen to two employees talk about their jobs. What does Leticia do? What does So do?

B With a partner, write examples of the two employees' behavior in the chart below.

Leticia	So
comes to work on time	

C In your opinion, who is the better employee? Why? Can you think of other examples of good and bad employee behavior?

LESSON **GOAL** ➤ **Compare employee behavior and attitudes**

D Read the conversation below. Look at the words in *italics*. Which are possessive adjectives and which are possessive pronouns?

Ellen: *My* boss is quite demanding and she always wants *her* reports on time.
Leticia: Yes, *your* manager is more demanding than *mine*.
Ellen: Yeah, but *yours* is less friendly.

E Study the chart. Which possessive pronouns have an *s* at the end? Which possessive adjectives and possessive pronouns are the same?

Possessive Adjectives and Possessive Pronouns		
Possessive adjectives	**Rule**	**Example sentence**
my, your, his, her, our, their	*Possessive adjectives* show possession of an object and come before the noun.	This is *her* office.
Possessive pronouns	**Rule**	**Example sentence**
mine, yours, his, hers, ours, theirs	*Possessive pronouns* show possession of an object and act as a noun.	This office is *hers*.

F Underline the possessive adjective in each sentence. Circle the possessive pronoun.

EXAMPLE: <u>My</u> sister's manager is generous, but <u>my</u> manager is more generous than (hers.)

1. Their job is boring, but our job is more boring than theirs.

2. My husband gets a good salary. His salary is better than mine.

3. My brother says his coworkers are friendly, but my coworkers are friendlier than his.

4. I like her manager, but mine is much more easygoing.

5. His office is clean, but ours is bigger.

LESSON **GOAL** ➤ **Compare employee behavior and attitudes**

 Circle the correct word in each sentence below.

EXAMPLE: She keeps (her) / hers) work space very clean.

1. She never eats at (her / hers) desk, but they always eat at (they / theirs).

2. That office is (you / yours).

3. (Theirs / Their) company has more employees than his.

4. That's (your / yours) book. Where is (my / mine) book?

5. We will give you (our / ours) proposal so you can compare it with (your / yours).

 Leticia and Ellen are comparing the people they work with.

Leticia: I think an ideal manager should be demanding.
Ellen: I agree. A manager shouldn't be too easygoing.

I What is an ideal manager like? What are ideal coworkers like? Use the adjectives from the box and have a conversation with your partner.

friendly	courteous	funny	serious	demanding	respectful
strict	quiet	interesting	ambitious	hardworking	patient
relaxed	intelligent	easygoing	lazy	opinionated	reserved

 Form groups of three or four students. Compare your jobs. Then, write four sentences about your group using possessive pronouns.

EXAMPLE: <u>Anita has a friendly manager, but Jun's manager is friendlier than hers.</u>

1._____

2._____

3._____

4._____

LESSON **2**

It's pay day!

GOAL ➤ Interpret a pay stub

A Discuss the following vocabulary with your classmates and teacher.

year-to-date	marital status	rate of pay
earnings	Medicare	social security
federal	net pay	state disability
gross pay	payroll ending date	tax deductions
401K	pre-tax deductions	

B Look at Leticia's pay stub. Find the vocabulary words from the box above.

Employee Name: Leticia Rosales
Check number: 0768
SS number: XXX-XX-XXXX

Marital Status: single
Payroll Begin/End Dates:
5/14/08-5/27/08

HOURS AND EARNINGS

Description	Rate of Pay	Hours/Units	Earnings
Hourly/ Day/Monthly	14.75	80	1,180.00

TAX DEDUCTIONS

Tax Description	Current Amount	Calendar Year-to-Date
Federal	102.78	205.56
State	19.72	39.44
Social Security	10.68	21.36
Medicare	14.29	18.58
State Disability		

PRE-TAX DEDUCTIONS

Description	Amount
401K	50.00
Current Total	50.00
Year-to-Date Total	100.00

	Gross Pay	Pre-Tax Deductions	Pre-Tax Retirement	Tax Deductions	Net Pay
urrent	1,180.00	50.00		147.47	982.53

 LESSON **2** **GOAL** ➤ **Interpret a pay stub**

C Where can you find this information on the pay stub? Write the number of each section of Leticia's pay stub.

Pay stub information	Section
1. weeks the paycheck covers	1
2. total amount she takes home	_____
3. information about retirement savings	_____
4. information about taxes	_____
5. hourly wage	_____

D Work with a partner to answer the questions about Leticia's pay stub. Student A looks at the pay stub. Student B asks the questions and writes the answers. Then, switch roles.

EXAMPLE: *Student A*: Is she married?
            Student B: No.

1. Did she pay into social security this month? _____

   If so, how much? _____

2. Does she pay Medicare? _____

3. Does she pay state disability insurance? _____

4. How much federal tax has she paid this year? _____

5. How much money did she make this month before taxes? _____

6. How much state tax did she pay this month? _____

7. What does she get paid per hour? _____

8. What is her social security number? _____

E Discuss these questions with a partner.

1. Would you rather get paid every week, twice a month, or once a month? Why?

2. Would you rather get paid a salary or get paid hourly? Why?

F   Skim So's pay stub and answer the questions below.

Employee Name: So Tran			
Check Number: 0498			
S.S. Number: 000-56-8976			
Marital Status: Married			
Payroll Begin/End Dates: 9/01/08–9/15/08			

Tax Deductions		
Tax Deductions	**Current Amount**	**Calendar Year-to-Date**
Federal	27.16	488.88
State	5.29	95.22
Social Security	6.68	126.92
Medicare	9.29	167.22
State Disability		

Hours and Earnings
Description: Hourly/Day/Monthly
Rate of Pay: 9.25
Hours/Units: 80
Earnings: 740.00

Pre-Tax Deductions	
Description	**Amount**
401K	25.00
Current Total	25.00
Year-to-Date Total	475.00

	Gross Pay	Pre-Tax Deductions	Pre-Tax Retirement	Tax Deductions	Net Pay
Current	740.00	25.00		48.42	666.28

1. Did So pay into social security this month? _____ If so, how much? _____

2. Does he pay Medicare? _____

3. Does he pay state disability insurance? _____

4. How many hours did he work during this pay period? _____

5. How much federal tax has he paid this year? _____

6. Does so contribute to a retirement account? _____ If so, how much? _____

7. How much money did he make this month after taxes? _____

8. How much money did he make this month before taxes? _____

9. How much state tax did he pay this month? _____

10. Is he married? _____

11. What does he get paid per hour? _____

12. What is his social security number? _____

LESSON 3

What are the benefits?

GOAL ➤ Interpret benefit information

A Read the list of benefits. Put a check mark (✓) next to the ones given at your present or last job. Add another benefit that you know.

❑ 401K

❑ bonus

❑ dental insurance

❑ disability insurance

❑ family leave

❑ health insurance

❑ daycare

❑ maternity leave

❑ medical leave

❑ overtime

❑ paid personal days

❑ paid sick days

❑ paid vacation days

❑ _____

CD 1
TR 16

B Benefits are extra things that a company offers its employees in addition to a salary. Listen to the career counselor talk about the benefits that three companies offer. Fill in the chart.

Company	Health/Dental insurance	Sick days	Vacation days	401K
Set-It-Up Technology	full medical and dental insurance			yes—$1 for every dollar you contribute
Machine Works				
Lino's Ristorante				yes—50¢ for every dollar you contribute

C Which company would you rather work for? Why? Discuss your answer with a partner.

D Read about the benefits offered by some local companies in a small town in Utah.

> ## Employment Monthly
> ### Your Source for Employment Information in Well Springs, Utah
>
> **First Marketing** offers medical benefits, including dental insurance, disability insurance, family leave, medical leave, and maternity leave to all full-time employees. You'll get paid for up to six sick or personal days you need to take. In addition to the great health benefits, you'll have the opportunity to contribute to a 401K as well as receive bonuses based on productivity at the end of the year. Most employees work full-time and receive time and a half for any overtime they work.
>
> **Quick Clean** is a large chain of cleaners and there are employment opportunities at local areas in your community. All full-time employees receive health insurance. You can pay extra for dental insurance, but Quick Clean offers medical and maternity leave. All employees receive a certain number of sick days as well as vacation days, based on how long they have been with the company. Quick Clean doesn't offer any bonuses or 401K plans, but they encourage their employees to meet with their financial planner to help plan for retirement.
>
> **Ernie's Electrical** offers medical, dental, maternity, disability, family, and medical leave to all full- and part-time employees. They give all of their employees three weeks a year to do with as they please—they can be used as sick days, personal days, or vacation days. No employees work overtime at Ernie's Electrical, which helps cut down on costs, but everyone receives a holiday bonus.

E Read about each person. Decide which company would be best for him or her.

1. Alicia is a young, hardworking student who can only work part time. She needs benefits because she lives by herself and has no family in Utah.

_____

2. Lars needs full benefits and likes to work overtime to make as much money as possible. He already has a 401K from another company that he would like to transfer to his new company.

_____

3. The most important thing for Su is maternity benefits. She and her husband are ready to start their family, but she still needs to work. She doesn't need dental insurance because her husband's company covers her.

_____

 LESSON 3   **GOAL** ➤ Interpret benefit information

F   **Complete the statements with a word or phrase from Exercise A on page 127.**

1. __Disability insurance__ is for those who get injured at work.

2. At times, employees need to take time to care for a sick family member. This is

   called _____.

3. Most companies are required to offer their employees _____
   to take care of them and their families when they are sick.

4. Some companies offer a retirement plan called a _____.

5. When a company shares its profits with the employees, each employee gets a

   _____.

6. When a woman has a new baby, she is allowed to take _____.

7. When you take a day off to do something for yourself, it is called a

   _____.

8. Some companies pay _____ when you work more than forty
   hours a week, or on weekends and holidays.

G   **With a group, imagine that you are starting a company. Decide what benefits you will offer. Answer the questions below.**

1. How many sick days will each employee receive? _____

2. How many personal days will you give each employee? _____

3. How many vacation days will each employee get? _____

4. Will you offer overtime pay? If yes, how much will you pay employees for

   overtime work? _____

5. What other benefits will you offer your employees? List them below.

   _____

   _____

GOAL ➤ Identify safe workplace behavior

A Look at the pictures below. What type of job does each person have? Who needs to consider health issues? Who needs to consider safety issues?

Minh

Arnie

Wassim

Robin

B Write the name of the person who should wear the safety items below.

1. a back support belt   _____

2. safety goggles   _____

3. earplugs   _____

4. a hairnet   _____

C Ask your partner if he or she wears safety items at work.

LESSON 4

GOAL ➤ Identify safe workplace behavior

D Read the conversation between Arnie and his manager, Fred. Do you think Fred is right?

Fred: Arnie, why aren't you wearing a back support belt?
Arnie: Oh, I don't need one.
Fred: If you don't wear a belt, you might get hurt.
Arnie: I don't think so. I'm really careful.
Fred: I know, but you could fall. Or you might lift something that is too heavy.
Arnie: You're right. If I get hurt, I might miss work. I could lose a lot of money if I can't work.
Fred: Exactly. Let me get you a belt.

E Underline the words *might* and *could* in the conversation above. Circle the verb that comes after each modal. Then, study the chart below.

Modals: *Could* and *Might*			
Subject	**Modal**	**Verb**	**Example sentence**
I, you, he, she,	could	fall	You could fall.
it, we, they	might	miss	I might miss work.
We use the modals *could* and *might* to say that there is a chance that something will happen in the future.			

F We also use *might* and *could* in conditional sentences with *if* when we are talking about possibilities. Complete the sentences.

EXAMPLE: If Arnie doesn't wear a back support belt, <u>he could get hurt.</u>

1. If Minh forgets to tie her hair back, _____.

2. José _____ if he doesn't wear a hard hat.

3. Wassim _____ if he doesn't wear safety goggles.

4. Robin _____ if he doesn't wear earplugs.

5. If Lilly doesn't buckle her seat belt, she _____.

Unit 7   Lesson 4   **131**

G Look at the safety hazards below. What's wrong in each picture?

1.

3.

2.

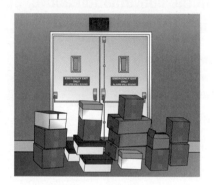

4.

H Write sentences about what *could* and *might* happen in the situations above.

1. _____

_____

2. _____

_____

3. _____

_____

4. _____

_____

I Work with a small group to make a list of safety rules for your classroom.

LESSON **5**

Good job!

GOAL ➤ **Communicate at work**

Vocabulary | Grammar
Life Skills
Academic | Pronunciation

A Look at the picture. Is the manager criticizing or complimenting her employee? What do you think they are saying?

> *criticize:* to say something negative
>
> *compliment:* to say something nice

B Identify the different types of communication. Write *compliment* or *criticism* next to each sentence below.

1. Good job!   _____compliment_____

2. You need to work a little faster. _____

3. You shouldn't wear that shirt to work. _____

4. That was an excellent presentation. _____

5. You are really friendly to the customers. _____

6. Please don't take such long breaks. _____

7. You are one of our best workers. _____

 CD 1 TR 17

C Are these people responding to criticism or a compliment? Write *compliment* or *criticism* next to each sentence below. Then, listen and check your answers.

1. Thanks. I'm glad to hear it. _____

2. I'm sorry. I'll try to do better next time. _____

3. Thanks. _____

4. I'm sorry. I won't wear it again. _____

5. Thank you. I appreciate your telling me that. _____

6. OK. It won't happen again. _____

D Use the sentences and responses in Exercises B and C to make conversations with a partner.

EXAMPLE: *Student A:* Good job!
                    Student B: Thank you. I appreciate your telling me that.

E Compare the two conversations. Then, study the charts.

Conversation 1

Employee: Excuse me. Would you mind looking over this report for me before I send it out?
Manager: Yes, of course. That's no problem.

Conversation 2

Susan: Could you give me a hand with this box?
Coworker: Sure, I'll be right over.

Polite Requests	
Would you mind helping me?	Polite and formal
Could you help me, *please*?	Polite and friendly
Can you give me a hand?	Polite and informal
Come here!	Very informal and impolite
When we speak to friends or colleagues, it is polite to be less formal. When we speak to a boss or a manager, it is polite to be more formal.	

Agree	Refuse
Sure.	No. I'm really sorry.
That's fine.	I'm sorry but I can't.
Of course.	I'd like to but I can't because . . .
No problem.	
Certainly.	

Pronunciation

Rising Intonation for Polite Requests

➤ Would you mind helping me?

➤ Can you give me a hand?

Tone of Voice for Agreeing and Refusing

➤ When you *agree* to something, your voice should sound *happy* and *upbeat*.

➤ When you *refuse* something, you should sound *apologetic*.

GOAL ➤ **Communicate at work**

CD 1
TR 18

F Listen to these people talking to their bosses, coworkers, and employees. Are they being impolite or polite? Check the correct answer.

1. ___ impolite   ___ polite   3. ___ impolite   ___ polite

2. ___ impolite   ___ polite   4. ___ impolite   ___ polite

G Complete the conversations below with a partner. Then, practice your conversations and present them to the class.

Conversation 1

A: That was an excellent project you turned in.

B: _____

A: I'm going to share it with all the other employees.

B: _____

Conversation 2

A: Please don't be late to work anymore.

B: _____

A: It's really affecting your work.

B: _____

Conversation 3

A: _____

B: Sure, I'd be happy to.

A: _____

H Work with a partner. Practice making and responding to polite requests, and complimenting and criticizing.

1. Your manager gave you a good employee review.
2. Ask your coworker to give you a ride home.
3. Your coworker is always late.
4. Ask your boss to help you check some accounts.

Review

A Work with a partner. Imagine that you need to hire several new employees for your business. Use the vocabulary from the box to talk about the qualities you are looking for. (Lesson 1)

EXAMPLE: *Student A:* I think an ideal employee is serious.
                       Student B: I agree. Good employees shouldn't be lazy.

friendly	courteous	funny	serious	demanding	respectful
strict	quiet	interesting	ambitious	hardworking	patient
relaxed	intelligent	easygoing	lazy	opinionated	reserved

B Circle the correct word in each sentence. (Lesson 1)

1. Have you seen (my / mine) new pen?

2. (They / Their) cafeteria has delicious food but (our / ours) is awful.

3. Can I use (your / yours) stapler? I can't find (my / mine.)

4. (Our / Ours) salary is low but we get a lot of tips.

5. (My / Mine) benefits are really good but (her / hers) are better.

C Match the description to the benefit. (Lesson 3)

Benefit	Description
___ 1. 401K	a. for work injuries
___ 2. bonus	b. a day off to do something for yourself
___ 3. disability insurance	c. time off to have a baby
___ 4. family medical leave	d. retirement savings
___ 5. maternity leave	e. a day off if you are sick
___ 6. personal day	f. when a company shares its profits
___ 7. sick day	g. time off to care for a sick family member

D **Skim Ali's pay stub and answer the questions below. (Lesson 2)**

Employee Name: Ali Ramsey		Marital Status: Single	
Check Number: 89765		Payroll Begin/End Dates	
S.S. Number: 000-89-2524		8/01/07–8/15/07	

HOURS AND EARNINGS			
Description	Rate of Pay	Hours/Units	Earnings
Hourly/Day/Monthly	11.75	56	658.00

TAX DEDUCTIONS		
Tax Description	Current Amount	Calendar Year-to-Date
Federal	17.65	141.20
State	6.75	54.00
Social Security	5.23	41.84
Medicare	3.26	26.08
State Disability	4.25	34.00

PRE-TAX DEDUCTIONS	
Description	Amount
401K	1005.00
Current Total	100.00
Year-to-Date Total	800.00

	Gross Pay	Pre-Tax Deductions	Pre-Tax Retirement	Tax Deductions	Net Pay
Current	658.00	100.00		37.14	520.86

1. Did Ali pay into social security this month? _____

   If so, how much? _____

2. Does Ali pay Medicare? _____

3. Does he pay state disability insurance? _____

4. How many hours did he work during this two-week pay period? _____

5. How much federal tax has Ali paid this year? _____

6. Does he contribute any money to a retirement account? _____

   If so, how much? _____

7. How much money did he make this month after taxes? _____

8. How much money did he make this month before taxes? _____

9. How much state tax did he pay this month? _____

10. What does he get paid per hour? _____

Review

E Complete the following sentences about work situations. Use a conditional with *might* or *could*. (Lesson 4)

1. If you don't mop the wet floor, _____.

2. If the truck driver drives too fast, _____.

3. If those construction workers don't wear earplugs, _____.

4. If the gardener doesn't wear gloves, _____.

5. If your manager sees you leaving early, _____.

6. If I quit my job, _____.

F Work with a partner. Practice responding to compliments and criticism using the sentences below. (Lesson 5)

EXAMPLE: *Student A:* You look very professional today.
Student B: Thanks. It's nice of you to say so.

1. Your report was excellent!

2. I noticed you were late again today.

3. Can you be a little neater with your work?

4. You finished that project so quickly!

G Work with a partner. Practice making and responding to polite requests using the situations below. (Lesson 5)

1. Ask your coworker to let you use her computer.

2. Ask your employee to send a fax.

3. Ask your coworker to help you lift a heavy box.

4. Ask your manager to give someone a message.

My Dictionary

Word Form: Parts of Speech

Use your dictionary to look up different word forms of vocabulary in this unit. Use the new word form in a sentence.

EXAMPLE: nouns: employee, employer   verb: __to employ_____

Our company wants to employ people with good computer skills.

1. noun: promotion   verb: _____

   _____

2. verb: to retire   noun: _____

   _____

3. verb: to commute   noun (person): _____

   _____

4. noun: accomplishment   verb: _____

   _____

Learner Log

In this unit, you learned many things about being on the job. How comfortable do you feel doing each of the skills listed below? Rate your comfort level on a scale of 1 to 4.

1 = Need more practice   **2** = OK   **3** = Good   **4** = Great!

Life Skill	Comfort Level	Page
I can compare employee behavior and attitudes.	1 2 3 4	_____
I can interpret a pay stub.	1 2 3 4	_____
I understand benefits.	1 2 3 4	_____
I can discuss workplace safety.	1 2 3 4	_____
I can respond to compliments and criticism.	1 2 3 4	_____
I can make and respond to polite requests.	1 2 3 4	_____

If you circled 1 or 2, write down the page number where you can review this skill.

Reflection

1. What was the most useful skill you learned in this unit? _____

   _____

2. How will this help you in life? _____

Create an employee handbook.

With your team, you will create one section of an employee handbook. With your class, you will create a complete employee handbook.

Employee Handbook
Table of Contents

Pay Stub Information **3**

Benefits **7**

Workplace Safety **19**

Workplace Communications **23**

1. Form a team with four or five students. Choose a position for each member of your team.

POSITION	JOB DESCRIPTION	STUDENT NAME
Student 1: Leader	See that everyone speaks English and participates.	
Student 2: Secretary	Write information for the handbook.	
Student 3: Designer	Design brochure layout and add artwork.	
Students 4/5: Member(s)	Help secretary and designer with their work.	

2. With your class, decide what will be in your employee handbook. (Look at the table of contents in the illustration above for ideas.) Decide what part of the handbook each team will create. (Lessons 1–5)

3. Create the text for your section of the employee handbook. (Lessons 1–5)

4. Create artwork for your section of the employee handbook.

5. As a class, create a table of contents and a cover. Put your handbook together.

6. Display your handbook so that other classes can see it.

Citizens and Community

GOALS

➤ Identify U.S. geographical locations

➤ Compare and contrast ideas

➤ Interpret the system of U.S. government

➤ Express opinions about community issues

➤ Write a speech

The United States

GOAL ➤ Identify U.S. geographical locations

A Look at the map of the United States. How many states are there? Find your state and circle it. Put an *X* on the states you have visited. Write the names of the cities in the spaces provided.

| Philadelphia | Los Angeles | Jamestown | New York | San Francisco | Houston |

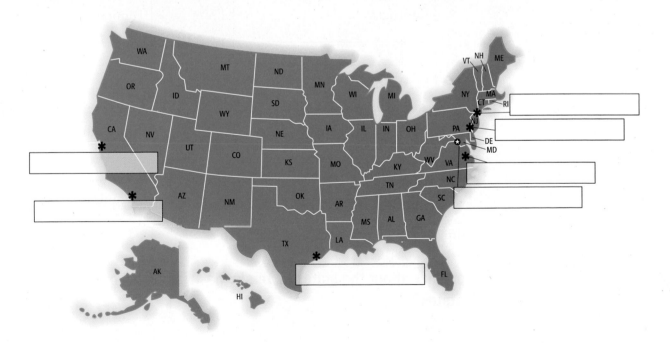

B Read the state abbreviations and write the full state name. Ask a classmate or your teacher if you need help.

AL	Alabama	MT	_____
AK	_____	NE	Nebraska
AZ	_____	NV	_____
AR	Arkansas	NH	New Hampshire
CA	_____	NM	_____
CO	_____	NJ	_____
CT	Connecticut	NY	_____
DE	Delaware	NC	North Carolina
FL	_____	ND	North Dakota
GA	_____	OH	_____
HI	_____	OK	Oklahoma
ID	_____	OR	_____
IL	Illinois	PA	_____
IN	Indiana	RI	Rhode Island
IA	_____	SC	_____
KS	_____	SD	_____
KY	Kentucky	TN	Tennessee
LA	_____	TX	_____
ME	_____	UT	_____
MD	Maryland	VT	_____
MA	_____	VA	Virginia
MI	Michigan	WA	Washington
MN	_____	WV	_____
MS	Mississippi	WI	_____
MO	Missouri	WY	Wyoming

Note: Washington, DC, is not a state.

C Ask your partner about the states he or she has visited. Who has visited the most states?

GOAL ➤ Identify U.S. geographical locations

D Look at the pictures of popular tourist attractions in the United States. What are they? Where are they located?

CD 1
TR 19

E Listen to the lecture on notable cities in the United States. Match the city on the right with the information on the left. Review the vocabulary with your teacher before you start.

Information	City
1. __g__ where the federal government is located	a. Houston, TX
2. _____ home of the Statue of Liberty	b. Jamestown, VA
3. _____ a major port for the Pacific Ocean	c. Los Angeles, CA
4. _____ an English colony named after an English king	d. New York, NY
5. _____ where the Declaration of Independence was written	e. Philadelphia, PA
6. _____ the film capital of the world	f. San Francisco, CA
7. _____ a major oil producer	g. Washington, DC
8. _____ where Disney World is located	h. Orlando, FL

F What else do you know about the cities listed above? Discuss your ideas with your classmates and teacher.

G What are some other cities in the United States? What are they known for? Include your own city or the city nearest you.

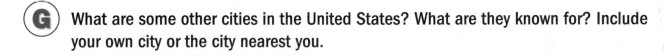

Which party?

GOAL ➤ **Compare and contrast ideas**

A The mayor is the top person in city government in most cities in the United States. Do you know who the mayor of your city is?

B Imagine that you are getting ready to vote for a new mayor of your city. Two candidates gave speeches about what is important to them. Read about their different points of view.

Kim Vo wants to . . .	Dawson Brooks wants to . . .
➤ build more parks.	➤ drill for oil on empty land.
➤ lower class size in elementary schools.	➤ increase number of teachers per classroom.
➤ lower the tuition at city colleges for immigrant students.	➤ raise the tuition at city colleges for immigrant students.
➤ spend tax dollars on wider sidewalks in neighborhoods.	➤ spend tax dollars to improve library facilities.
➤ increase the number of police officers who patrol the streets.	➤ spend money to retrain current police officers.
➤ offer job training programs for homeless people.	➤ offer incentives for individuals to start their own businesses.

C With a partner, compare the two candidates using *but* and *however*.

EXAMPLE: Kim Vo wants to build more parks, but Dawson Brooks wants to drill for oil on empty land.

Dawson Brooks wants to drill for oil on empty land; however, Kim Vo wants to build more parks.

D Write two sentences comparing Kim Vo and Dawson Brooks using *but* or *however*.

1. _____

_____

2. _____

_____

E Which candidate would you vote for? Why? Write a paragraph on a separate piece of paper.

 LESSON 2   **GOAL** ➤ **Compare and contrast ideas**

F Ask students what their feelings are about the topics below. Ask two students about each topic and fill in the chart. Ask: *How do you feel about . . . ?* Think of your own topic for the last question.

Name	Topic	Agree	Disagree
Enrico	increasing the number of students in our class	✓	
Liz			✓

Name	Topic	Agree	Disagree
	building more schools in our community		

Name	Topic	Agree	Disagree
	providing bilingual education for children		

Name	Topic	Agree	Disagree

 G Study the chart with your classmates and teacher.

Comparing and Contrasting Ideas		
If two people share the same opinion, use *both . . . and* or *neither . . . nor*.		
Both	Enrico **and** Liz	<u>want</u> to increase the number of students in our class.
Neither	Suzanna **nor** Ali	<u>wants</u> to increase the number of students in our class.
If two people don't share the same opinion, use *but* or *however*.		
Enrico agrees with bilingual education,	**but** Liz doesn't.	
Ali doesn't agree with bilingual education;	**however,** Suzanna does.	
Punctuation Note: Use a semicolon (;) before and a comma (,) after *however*.		

GOAL ➤ **Compare and contrast ideas**

H Complete each sentence with *both, and, neither, nor, but,* or *however.*

1. Neither Alicia _____ Hoa wants the city to build a school instead of a park.

2. _____ Kim and Su want to increase the number of hours that our class meets.

3. Jeeva thinks ESL students should be in class with native English speakers;

   _____, Adam thinks they should have their own class.

4. Bruno believes all children should study a second language, _____ Liza thinks children should only learn their native language.

5. _____ Lim nor Jeremy wants more homework.

6. Both Elizabeth _____ Parker want to do more writing in class.

I Look back at the information you collected on your classmates in Exercise F. Write sentences comparing their ideas.

1. _____

   _____

   _____

2. _____

   _____

   _____

3. _____

   _____

   _____

4. _____

   _____

   _____

U.S. government

GOAL ➤ Interpret the system of U.S. government

 A Look at the diagram of the three branches that make up the U.S. government. What do you know about them?

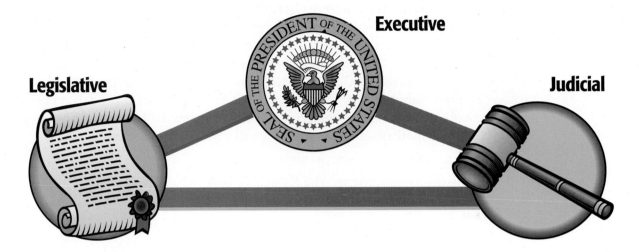

Legislative   **Executive**   **Judicial**

B Read about the U.S. government. Then, answer the questions after each section.

The U.S. Government

The U.S. government has three branches—the executive branch, the legislative branch, and the judicial branch. The government was set up this way so no one person would have too much power. With three branches, each branch balances out the others.

The Executive Branch

In the executive branch are the president, the vice president, and the cabinet. The president is the leader of the country and of the executive branch. He can sign new laws, prepare the budget, and command the military. The vice president helps the president and is the leader of the Senate. Both the president and the vice president serve for four years and can be reelected only once. The president's cabinet is a group of experts who advise the president. The president chooses his cabinet members. They include the Secretary of State, the Secretary of Defense, and the Secretary of Education.

1. What does the president do? _____

2. What does the vice president do? _____

3. How long do the president and vice president serve? _____

4. What does the cabinet do? _____

5. Are cabinet members elected? _____

GOAL ➤ Interpret the system of U.S. government

The Legislative Branch

The legislative branch, also known as Congress, makes the laws for the United States. Congress has the power to declare war, collect taxes, borrow money, control immigration, set up a judicial and postal system, and the most important power, to make laws.

This branch has the greatest connection to the people of the United States because this branch represents citizens. Congress has two parts—the House of Representatives and the Senate. The House of Representatives has 435 state representatives. Each state gets a certain number of representatives based on its population. Each representative serves for two years and can be reelected. The Senate has 100 senators, two from each of the 50 states. Senators serve for six years and can also be reelected.

1. What is another name for the legislative branch? _____

2. What does this branch do? _____

3. What are the two parts of this branch called? _____

4. How many representatives are in the House? _____

5. What determines the number of representatives each state gets? _____

6. How long do representatives serve? _____

7. How many senators does each state have? _____

8. How long do senators serve? _____

The Judicial Branch

The third branch of the U.S. government is the judicial branch, which includes the Supreme Court and the federal courts. The job of the courts is to interpret the laws made by the legislative branch. The Supreme Court is the highest court in the United States, and has nine judges called justices. The justices listen to cases and make judgments based on the Constitution and the laws of the United States. The president and Congress choose the justices of the Supreme Court.

1. What is the role of the judicial branch? _____

2. What is the highest court in the United States? _____

3. How does a person become a judge on the Supreme Court? _____

_____

GOAL ➤ Interpret the system of U.S. government

CD 1
TR 20

C Most cities have government officials who are elected to help run the city. Listen to the following people talk about their jobs and fill in the chart with their duties.

Official	Duties
Tax Assessor	1. helps county set tax rates 2. decides on the value of property
City Clerk	1. 2.
City Council Member	1. 2.
Superintendent of Schools	1. 2.
Mayor	1. 2.

D Discuss the positions in the chart above with a group. Which position would you most like to have? Why? Which one would you least like to have? Why? Write a paragraph below.

_____

_____

_____

_____

_____

_____

_____

_____

_____

_____

Community concerts

GOAL ➤ **Express opinions about community issues**

A Cherie lives in a small town in California, but it's not as nice as it used to be. Read about the problems in Cherie's community.

Hi, my name is Cherie. I live in a small community called Rosshaven in California. I moved here about ten years ago with my family because we wanted to live in a nice, safe community, but many things have happened in the past ten years.

First of all, the neighborhood schools are overcrowded. Because our school system is so good, many families from outside neighborhoods send their kids to our schools. There are over 35 students in each classroom.

Another problem is that there are many homeless people on our streets. It sometimes makes me nervous to have my kids walking home by themselves. I wish they could take a bus, but that's another problem. We don't have any public transportation here. When Rosshaven was first built, many wealthy people moved here. They all had cars, so there was no need for public transportation, but now things have changed. I think it's time for me to go to a city council meeting to see what I can do for our community.

B Cherie talks about three different problems in the reading above. List them below.

1. _____

2. _____

3. _____

LESSON 4 **GOAL** ➤ **Express opinions
about community issues**

C With a group, discuss possible solutions to each problem in Cherie's community. Write your ideas below. Report your answers to the class.

Problem	Possible solutions
	1. 2.
	1. 2.
	1. 2.

D Rosshaven is a nice place to live, but like every community, it has some problems. Match each problem with a possible solution. Then, compare answers with a partner and say if you agree or disagree with each solution.

Problem

_____ 1. Visitors park in resident parking spaces.

_____ 2. People don't clean up after their animals.

_____ 3. Teenagers are out late at night getting into trouble.

_____ 4. The parks are not well kept up.

Solution
The city council should . . .

a. set a curfew for teenagers.

b. fine people who don't clean up after their pets.

c. give tickets to visitors who park in resident spaces.

d. raise taxes to help with recreation improvements.

E We use *should* to give a strong suggestion. Study the chart below with your teacher.

Should			
Subject	**Modal**	**Base verb**	
The city council	*should*	set	a curfew for teenagers.
People	*should*	clean up	after their pets.

F With your group, use *should* to talk about the solutions you wrote in Exercise C.

G With a group, form a city council. Decide how you will solve the following problems and present your ideas to the class. The class will vote on which group would be the best city council.

1. There are no sidewalks on the busy streets in our town, and it is very dangerous. Many people get hurt because they walk too close to the cars. There is no space on the street to build sidewalks. What should we do to solve this problem?

   _____

   _____

   _____

   _____

   _____

2. The housing prices are going up in our community. It's difficult to find affordable rent and almost impossible to buy a house. Many people are moving away from the community to find cheaper housing. The community wants to maintain diversity, but only the very wealthy can afford to stay. What should we do about the housing costs?

   _____

   _____

   _____

   _____

   _____

3. The town's river was very dirty, but groups of citizens did a lot to clean it up. We want to increase taxes so we can build a new park along the river, but the growing town needs a new supermarket and more office space, too. Is there a way to make everyone happy?

   _____

   _____

   _____

   _____

   _____

LESSON 5 If I were president

GOAL ➤ Write a speech

Ⓐ Rosario's teacher asked her to write a paragraph about what she would do if she became president of the United States. Read what she wrote below.

> If I won the presidential election, I would be the first female president. If I were president, nobody would be poor or homeless. Personally, I think if people had more money, they wouldn't commit crimes. In my opinion, we shouldn't spend so much money on the military. If scientists didn't have to build weapons, they would have more time to study other things. Maybe they would find a cure for cancer. I think that I'd be a great president!

Ⓑ Study these expressions with your classmates and teacher. Underline the ones Rosario used in her paragraph above.

Expressing an Opinion

In my opinion, …   I believe that …

As I see it, …   I think that …

Personally, I think …   I feel that …

Ⓒ Write your opinion about the topics. Use the expressions from the box.

EXAMPLE: the environment

> I believe that the president of the United States should be more concerned about the environment.

1. homeless people

2. homework

3. public transportation in my city

4. learning English

Vocabulary Grammar
Life Skills
Academic Pronunciation

D Study the chart with your classmates and teacher.

	**Contrary-to–Fact Conditional Statements**					
If	**Subject**	**Past tense verb**	**Subject**	**Would**	**Base verb**	**Example sentence**
If	I, you, she, he, we, they	had / didn't have	I	would / wouldn't	buy	If I had more money, I would buy a new house
If	I, you, she, he, we, they	were / was / were't (wasn't)	I	would / wouldn't	spend	If I were (was) president, I would spend more money on education.
	*Contrary-to-fact (or unreal) conditional statements* are sentences that are not true and that the speaker thinks will probably never be true. **Note:** In written English, we use *were* instead of *was* in contrary-to-fact conditionals, but in spoken English we often use *was*.					

E Complete the sentences below with the correct form of the verbs in parentheses.

1. I ___would give___ (give) money to the homeless if ___I were___ (be) president.

2. If people _____ (have) more money, they _____ (be) happier.

3. If the president _____ (spend) more on health, scientists _____ (discover) a cure for cancer.

4. If our classes _____ (be) larger, the teacher _____ (not have) much time for each student.

5. Maria _____ (go) to medical school if she _____ (be) younger.

6. We _____ (walk) more if we _____ (drive) less.

F Look at the list of city officials on page 149. On a piece of paper, write a conditional statement for each official. Then, share your statements with a partner.

EXAMPLE: If I were the sheriff, I would hire more police officers. _____

G What would you do if you were president? Talk about the things you would like to change.

EXAMPLE: *Student A:* What would you do if you were president?
Student B: Let's see. I think we need to improve our schools.
Student A: How would you do that?
Student B: I would pay teachers more. I would spend money on things like computers.

H Think about the following topics. What would you do if you were president? Write your ideas.

Topic	My ideas
eliminating the death penalty	
raising the retirement age to 70	
raising the cost of gasoline so people would drive less	
smoking in public places	
raising the minimum wage	
building casinos to raise money for schools	

I Using the ideas you wrote above, write a paragraph about what you would do if you were president. Use Rosario's paragraph on page 153 as an example. Then, share your paragraph with the class. Who would the class elect to be president?

_____

_____

_____

_____

_____

_____

Review

 A Write the full name of each state next to its abbreviation. See how many you can remember before you look back at page 142. (Lesson 1)

1. NY _____   6. ME _____

2. CA _____   7. IL _____

3. WA _____   8. NV _____

4. FL _____   9. HI _____

5. TX _____   10. NJ _____

B Read the chart below. Write sentences using *both . . . and, neither . . . nor, but,* and *however.* (Lesson 2)

EXAMPLE: Both Sophia and Jamal want to increase class size. _____

Name	Topic	Agree	Disagree
Sophia	increasing the number of students	✓	
Jamal	in our class	✓	
Sophia	building more parks in the community		✓
Jamal		✓	
Sophia	hiring more police officers	✓	
Jamal			✓
Sophia	building more freeways		✓
Jamal			✓

1. _____

_____

2. _____

_____

3. _____

_____

C Check (✓) the correct branch of government after each statement. (Lesson 3)

	Legislative	Executive	Judicial
1. listens to cases and makes judgments			
2. interprets the laws			
3. signs new laws			
4. includes the president's cabinet			
5. includes the House of Representatives			
6. makes laws			
7. can control immigration			
8. commands the military			
9. includes the Congress			
10. chooses the justices of the Supreme Court			

D Look at the community problems below. Write a solution for each problem using *should*. (Lesson 4)

1. Problem: traffic on the freeways

   Solution: The city should build more carpool lanes.

2. Problem: smoking in parks near playgrounds

   Solution: _____

3. Problem: cars driving too fast in residential areas

   Solution: _____

4. Problem: potholes

   Solution: _____

5. Problem: high crime

   Solution: _____

Review

E Complete these contrary-to-fact conditionals with the correct form of the verbs in parentheses. (Lesson 5)

1. I _____ (work) faster if I _____ (have) a computer.

2. If she _____ (live) in Italy, she _____ (eat) pizza every day.

3. If it _____ (stop) raining, we _____ (play) outside.

4. If the town _____ (buy) more land, we _____ (build) schools.

5. I _____ (spend) more on education if I _____ (be) president.

6. If the president _____ (lower) taxes, he _____ (be) popular with Republicans.

7. People _____ (drive) less if gas _____ (be) more expensive.

8. If we _____ (prohibit) smoking in public places, everyone _____ (be) healthier.

F What would you do if you were mayor of your city? Write a paragraph stating your opinions about various local issues. Then, say what you would do if you were mayor. (Lesson 5)

EXAMPLE: In my opinion, the public transportation system in this town is very poor. The buses are always late because there is too much traffic. If I were mayor, I would build a subway system and . . .

_____

_____

_____

_____

_____

_____

My Dictionary

In this book, you have learned about ways to acquire vocabulary and use a dictionary. Now put everything together and practice writing an entry in a vocabulary book.

Word: 'legislature.
Part of speech: noun
Definition: a branch of the U.S. government that passes laws
Related word(s): legislation *(n)*, legislate *(v)*
Example sentence: The <u>legislature</u> passed a new law
                          on gasoline taxes.
Start a vocabulary notebook of your own. Add any new words
you have learned inside or outside of class. Start with a word or words from this unit.

Learner Log

In this unit, you learned many things about citizens and community. How comfortable do you feel doing each of the skills listed below? Rate your comfort level on a scale of 1 to 4.

1 = Need more practice   **2** = OK   **3** = Good   **4** = Great!

Life Skill	Comfort Level	Page
I can identify geographical locations in the U.S.	1 2 3 4	_____
I can compare and contrast ideas.	1 2 3 4	_____
I can talk about the U.S. system of government.	1 2 3 4	_____
I can discuss community issues.	1 2 3 4	_____
I can express opinions.	1 2 3 4	_____
I can write a speech.	1 2 3 4	_____

If you circled 1 or 2, write down the page number where you can review this skill.

Reflection

1. What was the most useful skill you learned in this unit? _____

_____

2. How will this help you in life? _____

Team Project

Create a flyer: Run for mayor.

With your team, you will run a mayoral campaign. You will write a list of community problems and your solutions, and create a flyer that will help you gain votes. You will also write a speech that you would give if you were elected mayor.

1. Form a team with four or five students. Choose a position for each member of your team.

POSITION	JOB DESCRIPTION	STUDENT NAME
Student 1: Leader	See that everyone speaks English. See that everyone participates.	
Student 2: Secretary	Write down the community problems, possible solutions, and the speech.	
Student 3: Designer	Create the flyer.	
Students 4/5: Members	Help the secretary and the designer with their work.	

2. Imagine someone on your team is running for mayor of your city. Answer the following questions:

   Why would you want to be mayor?

   Why would you be the best mayor?

3. Come up with a list of community problems and your solutions to those problems. (Lesson 4)

4. Create a flyer including all your information and any appropriate pictures or art.

5. Write a speech that you would give as mayor. (Lesson 5)

6. Present your flyer and speech to the class.

Stand Out 3 Vocabulary List

cardiovascular 94
cause 87
cavities 88
cholesterol 91
cold 86
conditions 82
desirable weight 93
digestion 92
diseases 82
dizzy 84
effect 87
exercise routine 93
fat 91
grain 91
fiber 91
habit 87
headache 84
healthy weight 93
ideal weight 93
ill 86
liver 87
lungs 87
maintain 93
moderation
nutrients 92
nutrients 92
organs 83
parts of the body (internal and external) 81-83
Physical fitness 93
protein 91
recreational 93
saturated 91
saturated fat 91
serving size 91
sick 86
sodium 91
sore 84
starch 91
stress 87
stroller 94
sugar 91
sunscreen 87
vitamins 92

Unit 6
assemble 104

abbreviations in job ads 107
career 101
character traits 113
connection 110
correction fluid 111
custodian 107
elderly 104
employment agency 110
enthusiasm 113
fax 107
hiring 110
insurance claim forms 107
job 101
job application 110
job titles 101-102
job training program 104
licensed 107
nursing home 107
operate 104
personality 113
position 110
practice 104
proof of car insurance 107
resume 110
self-confidence 113
sensitivity 113
sew 104
skills 102
supervisor 111
supplies 104
technician 107
title 102
warmth 113
wrinkle 111

Unit 7
401K 124
ambitious 123
back support belt 130
behavior 121
bonus 127
calendar 124
check number 124
compliment 133
courteous 123
coworker 122
criticism 133

current amount 124
current total earnings 124
demanding 123
dental insurance 127
disability insurance 127
dust mask 130
earplugs 130
easygoing 123
family leave
federal 124
gross pay 124
gloves 131
health insurance 127
health maintenance
hard hat 131
hairnet 130
ideal 123
life insurance 127
marital status 124
maternity leave 127
medical leave 127
Medicare 124
net pay 124
number 124
opinionated 123
overtime 127
patient 123
payroll ending date 124
payroll issue date 124
personal days 127
pre-tax 124
pre-tax deductions 124
protective 130
rate of pay 124
request 134
reserved 123
retirement 124
safety materials 130
safety goggles 131
seat belt 131
sick days 127
social security (SS)
state 124
state disability 124
strict 123
tax deductions 124
vacation days 127

year-to-date 124
year-to-date total 124

Unit 8
bilingual education 144
cabinet 147
casinos 155
capital 143
city officials 149
colony 143
Congress 148
controversial issues 144
curfew 150
drill for oil 144
executive 147
fine 150
homeless 150
House of Representatives 148
incentives 144
judicial 147
legislative 147
names of states 142
overcrowded 150
penalty 155
port 143
president 147
producer 143
resident 150
retirement 155
Senate 148
Supreme Court 148
tickets 150
tuition 144
vice-president 147
wage 155
wealthy 150

Stand Out 3 Irregular Verb List

The following verbs are used in *Stand Out 3* and have irregular past tense forms.

Base Form	Simple Past	Past Participle
be	was, were	been
become	became	become
break	broke	broken
build	built	built
buy	bought	bought
catch	caught	caught
choose	chose	chosen
come	came	come
do	did	done
drink	drank	drunk
drive	drove	driven
eat	ate	eaten
fall	fell	fallen
feel	felt	felt
fly	flew	flown
forget	forgot	forgotten
find	found	found
get	got	gotten
give	gave	given
go	went	gone
hang	hung	hanged/hung
have	had	had
hear	heard	heard
hold	held	held
hurt	hurt	hurt
keep	kept	kept
know	knew	known
learn	learned	learned/learnt
leave	left	left

Base Form	Simple Past	Past Participle
lend	lent	lent
lose	lost	lost
make	made	made
mean	meant	meant
meet	met	met
pay	paid	paid
put	put	put
read	read	read
ride	rode	ridden
run	ran	run
say	said	said
sell	sold	sold
shake	shook	shaken
show	showed	shown
sit	sat	sat
sleep	slept	slept
speak	spoke	spoken
spend	spent	spent
stand	stood	stood
take	took	taken
teach	taught	taught
tell	told	told
think	thought	thought
throw	threw	thrown
wake	woke	woken
wear	wore	worn
win	won	won
write	wrote	written

Comparatives

	Adjective	Comparative	Rule	Example sentence
Short adjectives	cheap	cheaper	Add -*er* to the end of the adjective.	Your computer was *cheaper* than my computer.
Long adjectives	expensive	more expensive	Add *more* before the adjective.	The new computer was *more expensive* than the old one.
Irregular adjectives	good bad	better worse	These adjectives are irregular.	The computer at school is *better* than this one.
Remember to use *than* after a comparative adjective followed by a noun.				

Superlatives

	Adjective	Superlative	Rule	Example sentence
Short adjectives	cheap	the cheapest	Add -*est* to the end of the adjective.	Your computer is *the cheapest*.
Long adjectives	expensive	the most expensive	Add *most* before the adjective.	He bought *the most* expensive computer in the store.
Irregular adjectives	good bad	best worst	These adjectives are irregular.	The computers at school are *the best*.
Always use *the* before a superlative.				

Must vs. *Have to*

Subject	Modal	Base verb	
We	have to	save	money for vacation.
I	must	pay off	my credit card every month.

Comparatives Using Nouns

Our new apartment has *more bedrooms* than our old one. Our old apartment had *fewer bedrooms* than our new one.	Use *more* or *fewer* to compare count nouns.
Rachel's apartment gets *more light* than Pablo's apartment. Pablo's apartment gets *less light* than Rachel's apartment.	Use *more* or *less* to compare noncount nouns.

Superlatives Using Nouns

Rachel's apartment has *the most bedrooms*. Phuong's apartment has *the fewest bedrooms*.	Use *the most* or *the fewest* for count nouns.
Rachel's apartment has *the most light*. Phuong's apartment has *the least light*.	Use *the most* or *the least* for non-count nouns.

Yes/No Questions and Answers with *Do*

Questions				Short answers
Do	Subject	Base verb	Example question	
do	I, you, we, they	have	Do they have a yard?	Yes, they do. / No, they don't.
does	he, she, it	want	Does she want air-conditioning?	Yes, she does. / No, she doesn't.

Information Questions

Question words	Example questions
How What When	*How* may I help you? *What* is your current address? *When* would you like your service turned off?

Past Continuous

Subject	*be*	Verb + *ing*	Example sentence
I, he, she, it	was	making	I was making breakfast.
you, we, they	were	studying	She was taking a shower.
Use the past continuous to talk about things that started in the past and continued for a period of time.			

Past Continuous Using *While*

Subject	*be*	Verb + *ing*	Example sentence
I, he, she, it	was	making	While I was making dinner, I saw a mouse.
you, we, they	were	studying	The electricity went out while we were studying.
To connect two events that happened in the past, use the past continuous with *while* for the longer event. Use the simple past for the shorter event. *Note:* You can reverse the two clauses, but you need a comma if the *while* clause comes first.			

Information Questions

Location	Where	is the bank?
	How far	is the school from here?
	What	is the address?
Time	When	does the library open?
	What time	does the restaurant close?
	How often	do the buses run?
Cost	How much	does it cost?

Adverbial Clauses with *Before, After* and *When*

EXAMPLE	RULE
After I returned the books, I stopped by the bank to make a deposit.	The action closest to *after* happened first. (First, she returned the books. Second, she went to the bank)
Before I went grocery shopping, I stopped by the cleaners to pick up some skirts.	The action closest to *before* happened second. (First, she went to the cleaners. Second, she went grocery shopping.)
When everyone left the house, I made my list of errands and off I went.	The action closest to *when* is completed and then next act begins. (First, everyone left. Second, she made her list.)
I went home **when** I finished shopping. **When** I finished shopping, I went home.	You can reverse the two clauses and the meaning stays the same. You need a comma if the adverbial clause goes first.

Present Perfect

Subject	*have*	Past participle		Time	Example sentence
I, you we, they	have	been	sick	since Tuesday	I *have been* sick since Tuesday.
she, he, it	has	had	a backache	for two weeks	She *has had* a backache for two weeks.
Use the present perfect for events starting in the past and continuing up to the present.					

Future Conditional Statements

Cause: *If* + present tense	Effect: future tense
If you *are* very stressed,	you *will have* high blood pressure.
If you *don't eat* enough calcium,	you *won't have* strong bones.

We can connect a cause and an effect by using a *future conditional* statement. The *if*-clause (or the *cause*) is in the present tense and the *effect* is in the future tense.

Effect: future tense	Cause: *if* + present tense
You *will have* high blood pressure	*if* you *are* very stressed.

You can reverse the clauses, but use a comma only when the *if*-clause comes first.

Infinitives and Gerunds
Infinitive = *to* + verb   Gerund = verb + *ing*

Verb	Infinitive or Gerund?	Example sentence	Other verbs that follow the same rule
want	infinitive	He wants *to get* a job.	plan, decide
enjoy	gerund	He enjoys *fixing* bicycles.	finish, give up
like	both	He likes *to talk*. He likes *talking*.	love, hate

Gerunds and Nouns after Prepositions

Subject	Verb	Adjective	Preposition	Gerund/Noun	Example sentence
I	am	good	at	calculating	I am good at *calculating*.
she	is	good	at	math	She is good at *math*.

A gerund or a noun follows an adjective + a preposition. Some other examples of adjectives + prepositions are *interested in, afraid of, tired of, bad at*, and *worried about*.

Would rather

Subject	*would rather*	Base form	*than*	Base form	Example sentence
I, you, she, he, it, we, they	would ('d) rather	work alone	than	work with people	I would rather work alone than work with people.

Note: You can omit the second verb if it is the same as the first verb.
Example: I would rather work nights than (work) days.

Possessive Adjectives and Possessive Pronouns

Possessive adjectives	Rule	Example sentence
my, your, his, her, our, their	*Possessive adjectives* show possession of an object and come before the noun.	This is *her* office.
Possessive pronouns	**Rule**	**Example sentence**
mine, yours, his, hers, ours, theirs	*Possessive pronouns* show possession of an object and act as a noun.	This office is *hers*.

Modals: *Could* and *Might*

Subject	Modal	Verb	Example sentence
I, you, he, she, it, we, they	could	fall	You could fall.
	might	miss	I might miss work.

We use the modals *could* and *might* to say that there is a chance that something will happen in the future.

Comparing and Contrasting Ideas

If two people share the same opinion, use *both . . . and* or *neither . . . nor*.		
Both	Enrico **and** Liz	want to increase the number of students in our class.
Neither	Suzanna **nor** Ali	wants to increase the number of students in our class.
If two people don't share the same opinion, use *but* or *however*.		
Enrico agrees with bilingual education,	**but** Liz doesn't.	
Ali doesn't agree with bilingual education;	**however,** Suzanna does.	
Punctuation Note: Use a semicolon (;) before and a comma (,) after *however*.		

Should

Subject	Modal	Base verb	
The city council	should	set	a curfew for teenagers.
People	should	clean up	after their pets.

Contrary-to–Fact Conditional Statements

If	Subject	Past tense verb	Subject	*Would*	Base verb	Example sentence
If	I, you, she, he, we, they	had / didn't have	I	would wouldn't	buy	If I had more money, I would buy a new house
If	I, you, she, he, we, they	were was / were't (wasn't)	I	would wouldn't	spend	If I were (was) president, I would spend more money on education.

Contrary-to-fact (or unreal) conditional statements are sentences that are not true and that the speaker thinks will probably never be true.

Note: In written English, we use *were* instead of *was* in contrary-to-fact conditionals, but in spoken English we often use *was*.

Stand Out 3 Listening Scripts

PRE-UNIT
CD 1, Track 1
Page P3
G. Listen to the greetings and responses.
A: Hi!
B: Hello.
A: Good morning!
B: Morning!
A: How are you today?
B: Fine.
A: How are you today?
B: Great!
A: How's it going?
B: Pretty good.
A: How are you doing?
B: OK.
A: How are you doing?
B: Not bad.
A: What's up?
B: Nothing.
A: What's new?
B: Not much.

CD 1, Track 2
Page P3
H. Now listen to the greetings and respond after each one.
Hi!
Good morning!
How are you today?
How's it going?
How are you doing?
What's up?
What's new?

UNIT 1
CD 1, Track 3
Page 5
E. Listen to Tuba and Lam. Identify their goals, obstacles, and solutions and write them in the spaces below.

My name is Tuba Kambriz. I came here from Afghanistan five years ago. My husband had to come here for business so my whole family moved here. Right now, we don't have enough money to pay the bills so my goal is to get a job to help my husband with money. But I have an obstacle—time. It will be difficult to work because I have to take care of the children and the house. One solution is to work part time while my children are in school. Another solution is to have my mother help out around the house and help take care of the children. If we all work together, we will achieve our goal.

I'm Lam and I came to the United States from Vietnam many years ago. I was a political prisoner during the Vietnam War and now I'm happy to be safe in America with my family. The most important people in my life are my grandchildren. My goal is to send my grandchildren to college. But there is an obstacle. We don't have enough money to send them to college. I want them to have the education I never did so I think it's very important for them to go to school. My wife thought of one solution. She suggested they apply for scholarships. This is a good idea because both girls are very smart. The girls came up with another solution. They said they could work part time while going to school. We have been saving every penny we can to help them. I hope everything works out in the end.

CD 1, Track 4
Page 10
C. Listen to the reading about study habits. Listen for good and bad study habits.

Good study habits can be very beneficial to you and your education. On the other hand, bad study habits can be harmful to your educational goals. First, let's talk about bad study habits.

Many people have very busy schedules and it is difficult for them to find time to study. One bad study habit is not studying before class. Another bad study habit is studying with distractions around, such as television, people talking, or loud music. A third bad habit is copying a friend's homework. These are just a few bad study habits, but you can easily change them into good study habits.

There are many ways that you can improve your study habits. First, set a time every day to study and try to study at the same time every day. Do not make appointments at this time. This is your special study time. Second, find a good place to study, a place that is quiet and comfortable so you can concentrate. Finally, do your homework on your own. Afterwards, you can find a friend to help you go over your work and check your answers.

CD 1, Track 5
Page 13
C. Listen to the lecture about time management. Listen for the main ideas.

Time management is important for several reasons. First of all, it helps you stay organized. Second of all, you can make sure you are accomplishing everything that needs to get done. And thirdly, you can make time for family and friends and things that matter most. One of the best ways to manage your time is to keep a schedule. First, write down everything you need to do in a week. This includes work, school, children, and other tasks. Then put each of these into a time slot. Of course, you have to follow your schedule. And most important, check things off once they have been completed. There are some easy ways to add more time to your day. One, wake up a few minutes earlier. Even ten or fifteen minutes will give you some extra time to study or do things around the house. Two, have your family or friends help you with things you need to get done. For example, having your children help you with the housework will help you finish twice as fast. Three, try doing two tasks at once. Instead of just eating lunch, eat lunch and review your verb tenses. We call this *killing two birds with one stone*! There are some other important things to consider about time management. First of all, remember the important people in your life. Did you put time in your schedule to visit them, write them a letter, or even call them? Also remember your values. If you value exercise, you must schedule time to exercise. And finally, you are the boss of your schedule. Don't let your schedule control you. Managing your time will give you several benefits in life. You will find that you have more free time. In addition, you will feel less stressed because you are more organized. Also, you will have time to see the people in your life who matter most. And lastly, you will feel better about yourself.

UNIT 2
CD 1, Track 6
Page 31
E. Listen to Terron and his wife, Leilani, talk about purchasing methods. Make a list of the things they *have to* do or *must* do.
Leilani: Terron, you must go to the ATM tomorrow because we are out of cash.
Terron: What do you need cash for?
Leilani: I have to get groceries and I need to pick up the dry cleaning.
Terron: We really have to get a credit card. That way, we don't have to keep pulling cash out of the ATM.
Leilani: Yes, but if we get a credit card, we must pay it off every month. I don't want monthly debt hanging over our heads.
Terron: I agree. I have to go into the bank tomorrow anyway to cash my check so I'll get a credit card application for us to fill out then.

UNIT 3
CD 1, Track 7
Page 44
B. Listen to the Nguyen family talk about their housing preferences. Check the boxes next to the things they would like to have in their new apartment.
Maryanne: I think it's time to move. This apartment is too small.
Vu: I'm making more money now. I think we can afford a bigger place.
Truyen: Alright! Now I can have my own room.

Maryanne: Not so fast. We are not that rich, but it is hard with all four of you sharing one room. We need one bedroom for the girls and one for the boys.
Vu: Yes. A three-bedroom would be perfect.
Truyen: I want two bathrooms. Nga and Truc take hours to do their hair!
Maryanne: We don't have air-conditioning. I want air-conditioning in the new place.
Vu: Air-conditioning would be really nice. It gets so hot in the summer.
Truyen: Can we get a pool, too?
Vu: Well, we don't really need a pool. (Pause) Well, let's try to find a place that has one.
Truyen: Don't forget we need a yard for the dog. We don't have one now.
Maryanne: Of course, we want a nice space for Fluffy.
Vu: Let's get the paper and start looking for a place today!

CD 1, Track 8
Page 48
C. Vu and his family are getting ready to move. Vu calls the electric company to speak to a customer service representative. Listen to the recording and write short answers for the following information.
Recording: Thank you for calling Texas Electric. Your call is very important to us. Please choose from the following options. For new service or to cancel your existing service, press 1. To report a problem with your service, press 2. If you have questions about your bill, press 3. For all other questions, press 4.
(Vu presses 1.) Thank you. Just one moment.
Representative: Hello, my name is Kristen. How may I help you?
Vu: Um, yes. My family is moving next week. We need to cancel our current service and get service in our new home.
Representative: What is your current address?
Vu: 3324 Maple Road.
Representative: Are you Vu Nguyen?
Vu: Yes.
Representative: When would you like the service turned off?
Vu: Next Wednesday, please.
Representative: And what is your new address?
Vu: 5829 Bay Road.
Representative: And when would you like the service turned on?
Vu: This Monday, please.
Representative: OK. Your current service will be turned off sometime between 8 and 12 on Wednesday the 12th. Your new service will be on before 8 on Monday morning the 9th. Is there anything else I can do for you?
Vu: No, that's it.
Representative: Thank you for calling Texas Electric. Have a nice day.
Vu: You, too.

CD 1, Track 9
Page 49
E. Read the conversation as you listen to the recording. Underline the information questions.
Recording: Thank you for calling Southern Texas Gas. Your call is very important to us. Please wait for the next available customer service representative.
Representative: Hello, my name is Liam. How may I help you?
Vu: Um, yes. My family is moving next week and we need to have our gas turned off here and get the gas turned on in our new home.
Representative: What is your current address?
Vu: 3324 Maple Road.
Representative: What is your name, sir?
Vu: Vu Nguyen.
Representative: When would you like the gas turned off?
Vu: Next Thursday, please.
Representative: And what is your new address?
Vu: 5829 Bay Road.
Representative: And when would you like the gas turned on in your new home?
Vu: This Monday, please.
Representative: OK. Your current service will be turned off sometime between 7 and 9 A.M. on Thursday the 11th, and your new service will be on before 8 on Monday morning, the 9th. Is there anything else I can do for you?
Vu: No, that's it.
Representative: Thank you for calling Southern Texas Gas. Have a nice day.
Vu: Thanks. You, too.

CD 1, Track 10
Page 50
C. Listen to Maryanne and Vu talk about their finances. Fill in the missing information.

Maryanne: Now that you are making more money, I think we need to make a new budget.
Vu: OK, let's talk about income first. With the raise, my income will be $3,000 a month.
Maryanne: Great! And with my part-time job, I'm still making about $1,000 a month.
Vu: OK, that's it for income. The rent for our new apartment is going to be $1,350 a month. It's a bigger place so our utilities are going to go up.
Maryanne: Yeah, I was thinking our gas bill will probably be around $40 a month and our electricity will be about $60. Especially with that air-conditioning.
Vu: That sounds about right. What about the phone, cable, and Internet?
Maryanne: Well, if we use the same companies, they will be the same.
Vu: Is the phone bill really $65 a month?

Maryanne: Yes, it's an average. It includes long-distance calls to your mom in Vietnam.
Vu: I see. How much do you spend on groceries each month?
Maryanne: About $450. That shouldn't change. Um, what do we spend on the car?
Vu: Good news. We paid off the loan last month. Now the only expense is gas and maintenance.
Maryanne: Right. Let's budget $150 for that.
Vu: OK, well. it looks like we've got some extra money. Let's talk about how we can use it.

UNIT 4
CD 1, Track 11
Page 61
A. Gloria and her family are new to the community. Read her list of things to do. Where does she need to go for each one? Listen and write the names of the places below.

Gloria is new to the community. First of all, she needs to go to a bank to open a checking account so she can pay her bills. Second, she needs to go the Department of Motor Vehicles to register her car and renew her driver's license. For now, she will need to use public transportation, but she doesn't know where to get a bus schedule. She'll have to ask at the bus station. Also, she would like to take some ESL classes to improve her English. There is a community college nearby; maybe she could try there. Her children would like to play sports so she needs to find a place for them to do that. Perhaps she can call the Department of Parks and Recreation. Also, the kids want to use computers to e-mail their friends from the old neighborhood. They'll probably have the Internet at the public library.

UNIT 5
CD 1, Track 12
Page 91
D. Listen to Darla explain nutritional information to her grandmother.

Part 1
Grandma: Darla, I need your help.
Darla: Sure .What can I do, Grandma?
Grandma: Well, my doctor says I need to pay attention to nutrition, but I don't understand nutritional labels.
Darla: Oh, sure, I can help. Let's look at this box of macaroni and cheese. What's your first question?
Grandma: Well, I have high blood pressure. I shouldn't have a lot of salt. I don't see salt on this label.
Darla: Oh, you need to look at sodium. The sodium amount tells you how much salt there is.
Grandma: So, there is 470 mg of sodium in this box?
Darla: No, the amount they give you is the amount in each serving.

Grandma: How do I know how much a serving is?

Darla: They tell you on the label. See the serving size?

Grandma: OK. I see there are two servings in this box, one for me and one for grandpa.

Darla: What's next?

Grandma: I need to watch calories if I want to lose weight. How many calories should I have each day?

Darla: About 2,000. You can have more calories if you are active.

Part 2

Grandma: What should I eat if I want to have a healthy heart?

Darla: You should avoid cholesterol and saturated fat.

Grandma: OK. Grandpa is diabetic. He needs to limit sugar.

Darla: Yes, sugar is on the nutritional label.

Grandma: Now, Grandpa and I both need something to help digestion.

Darla: You need a lot of fiber.

Grandma: One last question. Why do older women need to have a lot of calcium?

Darla: Oh, that's because women need calcium to protect them against bone disease.

Grandma: That's really helpful. Thanks, Darla.

UNIT 6
CD 1, Track 13
Page 111
F. Read the rules for filling out an application below. What words could go in the blanks? Now listen and fill in the missing words.

Rules for Filling Out an Application

1. Use a dark pen—blue or black ink.
2. Don't cross out any mistakes. Use correction fluid to correct any mistakes.
3. Answer every question. If the question doesn't apply to you, write *NA—Not Applicable.*
4. Tell the truth! Never lie on your job application.
5. Don't bend or wrinkle the application.
6. Keep the application clean—no food or coffee stains!
7. Write as neatly as possible. Type it if you can.
8. If you don't understand the question, ask someone before you answer it.

CD 1, Track 14
Page 113
B. During a job interview, an employer will try to find out about an applicant's character and personality. Read and listen to find out what interviewers look for during an interview.

Your job interview is the most important part of the application process. This is when the employer gets to meet you and learn more about you. Employers are interested in your skills and experience, but they also look for personality and character traits.

Do you stand tall and smile confidently? Employers will notice your self-confidence. Managers want to hire employees who have confidence in themselves and will have confidence in the job they are doing.

Do you like to work hard and do a good job? Another important thing an interviewer looks for is enthusiasm about work. People who are enthusiastic about a job make great employees. They are happy with the work and usually stay with the company for a while.

Are you friendly and easy to talk to? Do you pay attention to how other people are feeling? Warmth and sensitivity are also very important traits. A person with these characteristics will make a good coworker, someone who can work well with others.

Do you have some or all of these traits? Can you show that you have these traits in an interview? If the answer is yes, you will have a good chance of getting the job.

UNIT 7
CD 1, Track 15
Page 121
A. Listen to two employees talk about their jobs. What does Leticia do? What does So do?

Leticia: Hi. I'm Leticia. I work for New Wave Graphics as an administrative assistant. I really like my job. I come to work on time every day and I never leave early. I try to keep my work space very clean and I never eat at my desk. When my manager asks me to do something, I get it done as soon as I can. I obey all the company policies, especially the safety rules. I try to be friendly to everyone I work with, even when I'm having a bad day. I am constantly learning new computer skills, so I can be ready to move up the ladder when a position becomes available. New Wave Graphics is a great company to work for and I hope to stay here a long time.

So: Hey, I'm So. I stock shelves at Johnson's Market. I'm supposed to come in at twelve and leave at eight, but I figure as long as I get my work done, it doesn't matter what time I get there. I've got long hair and my manager always tells me to keep it back, but he's never around, so I usually leave it down. It's my hair. I should be able to wear it how I want, shouldn't I? The best part about this job is the food. I stock the shelves with all the dry goods, such as cereal, crackers, and pasta. And there's always some extra stuff that doesn't fit on the shelves, so I usually take a few things home with me. I figure they should be paying me more for all the work I do, so I take a few things home to make up for it. I don't really like the guys I work with. They try too hard to impress the manager, so that they can get raises. I try to stay away from them and just get my work done as fast as I can. It's an OK job. I'll find something better soon.

CD 1, Track 16
Page 127

B. Benefits are extra things that a company offers its employees in addition to a salary. Listen to the career counselor talk about the benefits that three companies offer. Fill in the chart.

Career Counselor: Hello, future employees. My name is Kevin Daly and today's workshop is on company benefits. Can someone tell me what benefits are?

Participant: That's when the company pays for you to go to the doctor.

Career Counselor: Yes, that's true, but companies offer more than just health benefits. To give you an example of the different types of benefits that companies offer their employees, I'm going to talk about three different companies.

The first company is Set-It-Up Technology. This company helps small businesses set up computers in their offices. Their employees work six days a week, but they are paid a good salary. All employees are given full medical and dental insurance. In addition, employees are given twelve sick days and two weeks vacation a year. But the best benefit this company offers is its 401K retirement account. The company will match every dollar an employee contributes to the account.

The second company I'd like to talk about is Machine Works, an assembly plant that makes sewing machines. This company offers its full-time employees health benefits. There is no dental insurance. Machine Works gives their employees one week of sick leave and one week of vacation. This company pays a generous amount of overtime but there is no 401K offered by Machine Works.

The final company I'm going to talk about is Lino's Ristorante. This is a big chain restaurant so their benefits are pretty good. Employees receive health insurance but no dental benefits. Full-time employees receive eight sick days a year. All employees are given one week of paid vacation time every year. Lino's offers a 401K plan and they will contribute fifty cents for every dollar that you contribute.

So, these are some examples of benefits that different companies offer. Are there any questions?

CD 1, Track 17
Page 133

C. Are these people responding to criticism or a compliment? Write *compliment* or *criticism* next to each sentence below. Then listen and check your answers.

1. **A:** That was an excellent presentation!   **B:** Thanks, I'm glad to hear it.
2. **A:** You need to work a little faster.   **B:** I'm sorry. I'll try to do better next time.
3. **A:** You are a talented salesperson.   **B:** Thanks.
4. **A:** You shouldn't wear that shirt to work.   **B:** I'm sorry. I won't wear it again.
5. **A:** You are one of our best workers.   **B:** Thank you. I appreciate your telling me that.
6. **A:** Please don't take such long breaks.   **B:** OK. It won't happen again.

CD 1, Track 18
Page 135

F. Listen to these people talking to their bosses, coworkers, and employees. Are they being impolite or polite? Check the correct answer.

1. Bob, could you come to my office for a minute?
2. Give me that hammer.
3. Hey, we need more coffee.
4. Would you mail this package?

UNIT 8
CD 1, Track 19
Page 143

E. Listen to the lecture on notable cities in the United States. Match the city on the right with the information on the left. Review the vocabulary with your teacher before you start.

Now that we've talked about various states in the United States, I'd like to tell you about a few important cities. I'll start with one that really isn't called a city, but it's definitely very important—Washington, DC. *DC* stands for *District of Columbia*, which is what it is, a district. This is where the federal government is located: the White House, the Capitol building, and the Supreme Court.

Historically, two of the most important cities are Jamestown and Philadelphia. When the settlers first came from England in the 1600s, they came to Jamestown, Virginia, and named this first colony after King James of England. Many years later, the representatives of the thirteen colonies declared themselves an independent nation and wrote the Declaration of Independence in Philadelphia, which was the same place the Constitution was written.

Also on the East Coast, New York City was established. This is where European immigrants first came. They came to an island off the coast of New York called Ellis Island. Also off the coast of New York is Liberty Island. Liberty Island is the home of the Statue of Liberty, which was given to the United States by France in 1886.

Other famous cities include San Francisco, Los Angeles, and Houston. San Francisco, where the famous Golden

Gate Bridge is located, was one of the first established cities in California because it was a port for ships coming in from the Pacific Ocean. Los Angeles became the film capital of the world in the mid 1900s and has grown ever since. And finally Houston, Texas, put itself on the map by being one of the largest oil producers in the United States.

And who could forget Mickey Mouse, Donald Duck, and the whole Disney gang? Yes, Disneyland is in California, but Disney World is located in Orlando, Florida.

These are some of the most notable cities in the United States. Can you think of some other notable cities?

CD 1, Track 20
Page 149
C. Most cities have government officials who are elected to help run the city. Listen to the following people talk about their jobs and fill in the chart with their duties.

1. Hi, my name is Jim, and I'm the tax assessor. I help set tax rates by deciding the value of property. Some people don't like me because they think I cause higher taxes, but I'm just doing my job.

2. Hello there, I'm Su Young. I'm the city clerk. As city clerk, I keep track of records of property, local businesses, and registered voters. I also issue birth certificates and marriage licenses. So, if you're going to get married or have a baby, come see me!

3. I'm Christopher Erikson, a city council Member. I help to represent this community. All the council members meet with the mayor to discuss and solve community problems. It's really important to help make our community a better place to live.

4. Hi, my name is Sheryl, and I'm the superintendent of schools. I oversee the city schools and I help them do their job to provide a good education to our children. It's a very important job!

5. My name is Matt Peterson, and I'm the mayor of this town. I'm the head of the city government and I work with all the city council members to keep our community strong and happy.

Photo Credits

ACADEMIC SKILLS

Brainstorming, 73

Charts, tables, and maps, 6, 12, 15, 22, 26, 28, 29, 31, 42, 45, 51, 54, 62, 64–66, 67–69, 77, 85, 88, 105, 106, 114, 115, 122, 127, 141, 145, 154, 156

Drawing

Maps, 77

Grammar

Adverbial clauses, 71–72

Adverbs, 2

be, 54

Comparative adjectives, 28, 37, 42, 56

Conditional statements, 154

Contrary-to-fact conditionals, 154, 158

could and *might*, 131

Frequency adverbs, 2, 16

Future conditional statements, 88–89

Future time clauses, 6

Gerunds, 105, 106

Infinitives, 105

Information questions, 62–63

Modals, 131

must vs. *have to*, 32, 38

Past continuous, 54, 58

Past participles, 84

Possessive adjectives, 122

Possessive pronouns, 122

Prepositions, 106

Present perfect, 85

Requests, 134

Sequencing transitions, 34, 38

should, 151

Superlatives, 29, 37, 42

Verbs, 54, 84, 85, 105

while, 54

Writing, 16

Yes/No questions, 45–46

Group activities, 6, 26, 31, 40, 52, 60, 80, 100, 103, 120, 129, 132, 140, 152, 160

Listening

Attitudes at work, 121

Bill paying, 48

Communication at work, 135

Conversations, 49, 92, 134

Goals, obstacles, and solutions, 5

Greetings, P3

Housing, 44

Job interviews, 113

Purchasing methods, 31

Study habits, 10

Time management, 13, 14

U.S. geography, 143

U.S. government, 149

Matching

Diseases, 83

Doctors, 82, 96

Employee benefits, 136

Health habits, 87

Job applications, 110

Job descriptions, 102

Problems and solutions, 151

Questions and answers, 62

Study habits, 12

U.S. geography, 143

Partner activities, 1–2, P2, P3, 7, 23, 28, 31, 41, 43, 46, 53, 55, 61, 63, 78, 82, 86, 93, 101, 103, 113, 115, 125, 135, 138

Pronunciation

Focus, 3

Human body, 83

Information questions, 48a, 62

Making requests, 134

Phrasing, 72

Word stress, 119

Reading

Abbreviations, P7, 41

Advertisements, 24, 26, 36

Bill paying, 47

Charts, 6, 15, 22, 28, 29, 45, 54, 62, 64–66, 85, 88, 105, 106, 115, 122, 145, 154, 156

Classified Ads, 41, 56

Community issues, 150

Comparing information, 76

Conversations, P3, 84, 122

Daily activities, 70

Directions, 68–69

Educational goals, P7

Employee benefits, 127–129

Fitness information, 93–95, 97

Goals, 4

Goals, obstacles, and solutions, 8

Help wanted ads, 107, 109, 117

Housing, 44

Illnesses and symptoms, 84

Information questions, 49

Job applications, 111

Job interviews, 113

Job skills and preferences, 116

Letters, 55

Lists, 61

Maps, 67–69, 141

Nutrition labels, 90–92, 98

Outlines, 14

Pay stubs, 124–126, 137

Personal information, P4, P5

Purchases, 33

Schedules, 1

State abbreviations, 142

Study habits, 11

Tenant rights, 54, 55

Time management, 13

U.S. government, 147–148, 157

Workplace safety, 131

Speaking

Asking questions, 43, 45–46, 63, 64, 145

Bill paying, 47

Community issues, 152

Conversations, 53, 61, 63, 103, 110, 135

Doctors, 82

Goals, obstacles, and solutions, 5

Government officials, 149

Illnesses and symptoms, 84, 86

Introductions, P2

Job applications, 110

Jobs and careers, 101

Making comparisons, 28

Making requests, 134, 135

Partner activities, 1–2, 31

Purchasing methods, 31

Schedules, 1–2

Vocabulary

Adjectives, 123, 136

Adverbial clauses, 71–72

Advertisements, 24

Banks, 64

but and *however*, 144

Character traits, 114

Clothing and appearance, 114

Comparative adjectives, 28, 42

compliment and *criticize*, 133

Computers, 27

Contractions, P2, 4

could and *might*, 131

Directions, 68, 69

Employee benefits, 127

Fitness information, 94

for and *since*, 85–86

Frequency adverbs, 2

Goals, obstacles, and solutions, 4–5, 18

Health habits, 87

Human body, 81–83

Jobs and careers, 102

Job skills and preferences, 104

Opinions, 153

Pay stubs, 124

Possessive adjectives, 122

Possessive pronouns, 122

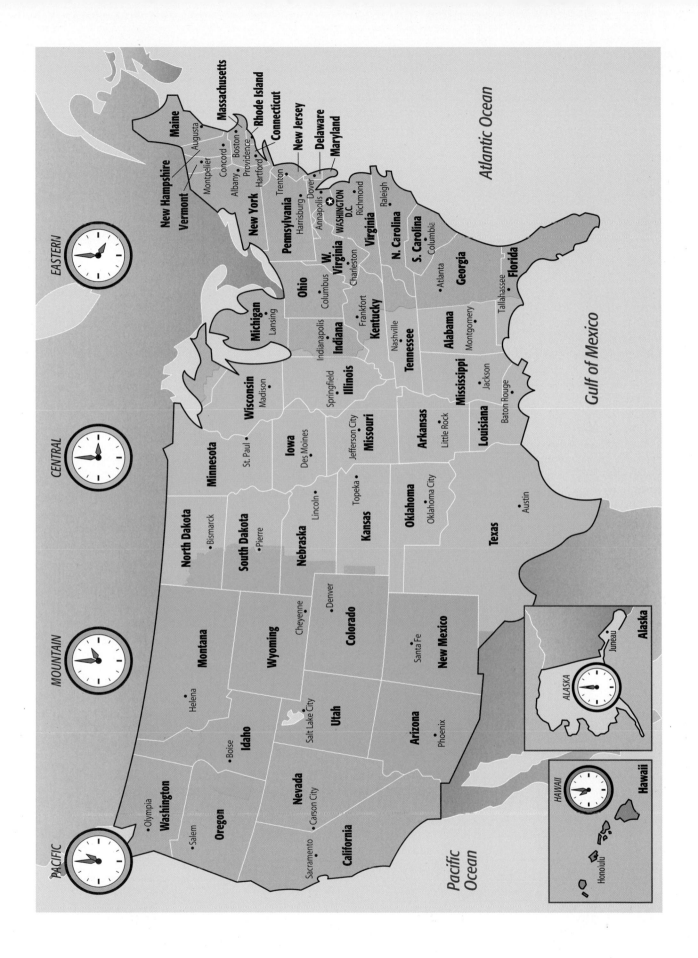